A PRACTICAL GUIDE TO CONSTRUCTION LENDING

Richard Ridloff

VNR VAN NOSTRAND REINHOLD COMPANY
——————————————————— New York

Copyright © 1985 by Van Nostrand Reinhold Company Inc.

Library of Congress Catalog Card Number: 84-11833
ISBN: 0-442-28225-7

All rights reserved. No part of this work covered by the copyright hereon may be reproduced or used in any form or by any means—graphic, electronic, or mechanical, including photocopying, recording, taping, or information storage and retrieval systems—without permission of the publisher.

Manufactured in the United States of America

Published by Van Nostrand Reinhold Company Inc.
135 West 50th Street
New York, New York 10020

Van Nostrand Reinhold Company Limited
Molly Millars Lane
Wokingham, Berkshire RG11 2PY, England

Van Nostrand Reinhold
480 Latrobe Street
Melbourne, Victoria 3000, Australia

Macmillan of Canada
Division of Gage Publishing Limited
164 Commander Boulevard
Agincourt, Ontario M1S 3C7, Canada

15 14 13 12 11 10 9 8 7 6 5 4 3 2 1

Library of Congress Cataloging in Publication Data

Ridloff, Richard.
   A practical guide to construction lending.

   Includes index.
   1. Real estate development—Finance—Law and legislation—United States. 2. Loans—Law and legislation—United States. 3. Construction industry—Finance—Law and legislation—United States. I. Title.
KF5698.3.R5   1984   346.7304′3   84-11833
ISBN 0-442-28225-7   347.30643

This book is dedicated to my wife Caren, and my two sons, Michael and Daniel for their patience and understanding, and to my parents, Sol and Daisey for their encouragement and years of sacrifice to finance my education.

Preface

There are a myriad of books in print covering various aspects of real estate development. Some of these books focus upon construction lending. However, none of them go beyond mere rhetoric and take you behind the scenes to the lender's domain.

One of the major stumbling blocks to commercial development has been the failure of the borrower/developer and lender to properly communicate with each other. Many developers simply do not understand lender requirements or are not properly briefed by the lender on how certain information should be presented so as to expedite the lender's review of submitted material. The result is oftentimes chaos. Loan closings are delayed and requests for advances are not processed in timely fashion, giving rise to even higher construction costs and disgruntled contractors.

This book attempts to rectify this communications problem by setting forth in detail lender requirements in the construction lending area. From the loan application stage through the issuance of the construction loan commitment to the payoff and satisfaction of the construction loan, lender practices are analyzed and examined with the result that borrower/developers should no longer be in a position to say "if only you'd told me what you wanted months ago."

The book will provide borrower/developers with insights into lender practices that only seasoned developers have at the present time and will serve as a reference guide to lenders themselves. Both attorneys and their clients will find the book useful, as will those individuals who are thinking of entering the real estate field. This is especially true of would-be real estate developers, loan officers and attorneys.

Richard Ridloff

Acknowledgment

Grateful acknowledgment is extended to Thomas P. Walsh and Zachary H. Wolff for all their assistance in reviewing the manuscript and giving me helpful suggestions. Sincere thanks is also extended to all those borrower/developers, attorneys and co-workers with whom I have transacted business, in particular Lloyd H. Reed and Norcross (Pete) Teel, Jr. Each experience has been a rewarding one and has contributed to the accumulation of knowledge that made this book possible.

Contents

Preface / vii

1. INTRODUCTION / 1

Construction Lending in the 1970s / 1
  The REIT Story / 1
  Others / 3
  The Late 1970s / 4
  Summary / 6
Construction Lending Today / 6
  Criteria / 6
  Take-out Commitment / 7
  Source of Financing / 7
  Industrial Development Bond Financing / 8
  New Activity / 9
  Summary / 13
Update 1984 / 13
Construction Lending Tomorrow / 17
  Interest Rates / 17
  Inflation / 17
  Decentralization / 18
  Migration / 18
  Population and Household Profiles / 18
  Energy / 19
  Other Factors / 19
  Growth Patterns / 19
  Summary / 20

2. LOAN UNDERWRITING / 22

The Application Process / 22
  The Lender's Staff / 22
  Lending Policy / 22
  Initial Screening Process / 23
The Underwriting Process / 23
  Economic Viability of the Project / 23
  Project Costs / 25
  Take-Out Financing / 26
  Risk Factor / 27
Credit Analysis / 27
  Net Worth Requirements / 28
  Verification of Net Worth / 28
  How to Read a Financial Report / 28
  Conclusion / 30
The Role of the Construction Architect/Engineer
in the Loan Underwriting Process / 30
  Cost Estimates / 31
  Plans and Specifications / 32
The Role of the Lender's Attorney
in the Loan Underwriting Process / 33
  Doing Business Requirements / 33
  Usury / 33
  Governmental Approvals / 34
  Take-Out Commitment / 34
  Other Matters / 34

3. STRUCTURING THE CONSTRUCTION LOAN / 36

Factors to Be Considered / 36
  Nature of Proposed Project / 36
  Borrowing Entity and Usury Problems / 37
  Borrower's Interest / 37
  Costs to be Financed / 37
  Method of Advancing Funds / 38
  Equity Requirements for the Borrower / 38
  Permanent Financing / 39
  General Contract / 39
  Major Subcontracts / 40

CONTENTS xi

  Government Approvals / 40
  Security for the Loan / 40
  Special Events of Default / 41
  Potential Title Problems / 41
  Other Factors / 41
 Selected Problems / 41
  Nonqualified Costs / 42
  Priority versus Mechanics' Liens / 42
  Contracts to Which the Lender Is Not a Party / 43
  Matters Over Which the Borrower Has No Written
    Contractual Control / 43
  Permanent Take-Out Commitment / 44
  The Time When the Project Is Almost Completed / 45
  Leasehold Loans / 45

4. LOAN PARTICIPATIONS / 47

 Why Participate? / 47
  Advantages to the Lead Lender / 48
  Advantages to the Participants / 49
 Commitment / 50
 Participation Certificate / 51
 The Participation Agreement / 51
  Percentage Interest in the Loan / 51
  Disbursement of Loan Proceeds / 52
  Representations and Warranties / 53
  Servicing / 53
  Assignment / 54
  Default by the Borrower / 54
  Default by either Party to the Participation Agreement / 55
  Other Provisions / 56
  Form of Agreement / 56

5. THE CONSTRUCTION LOAN COMMITMENT / 66

 A Sample Commitment / 66
 The Amendment Process / 74
  Guarantees / 75
  Lender Approvals / 76
  Fast Track Construction / 76

Calculating Advances / 77
Conclusion / 77

6. PREPARATION FOR LOAN CLOSING / 85

Legal Requirements / 85
Business Requirements / 95
  Forms / 95
  Appraisal / 96
  Final Plans and Specifications / 96
  Borings and Soil Reports / 96
  Detailed Cost Breakdown / 97
  Hazard and Casualty Insurance Policies / 97
  Labor and Material Payment and Performance Bonds / 97
  Draw Request / 98
  Letter of Credit / 98
  Closing / 99

7. TITLE INSURANCE AND MECHANICS' LIENS / 120

Title Insurance Coverage / 120
  Insurance Available / 120
  Amount of Insurance / 129
  Title Insurance Policies / 129
  Title Insurance Companies / 130
The Construction Mortgage versus the Mechanic's Lien—
A Question of Priority / 131
  Nature and Scope of Mechanics' Liens / 131
  Two Types of Legislation / 131
  Legislative Requirements / 134
  Priority of Lien / 134
  Title Insurance / 136
  Precautionary Measures / 137
  Bonding / 137
  State Survey / 137
  Conclusion / 138

8. THE PERMANENT TAKE-OUT COMMITMENT / 148

Forms of Take-Out Commitments / 148
  Interest Rate Adjusted and Additional Interest Mortgages / 148
  Land Purchase Leasebacks / 149

Dear Ed,

It was good seeing you again in Boston after the lapse of so many years since our college fraternity days. It was fortunate that our present interests coincide and that we work well together on the various deals that we have shared since that memorable day in Boston. I look forward to strengthening our ties and sharing future successes together. Cordially,

Your fraternity brother,

Rich

A PRACTICAL GUIDE TO CONSTRUCTION LENDING

Partnership Interests / 149
Prebuys / 149
Conventional Mortgages / 150
The Take-Out Commitment from the View
of the Construction Lender / 150
The Buy-Sell or Tripartite Agreement / 157
  Borrower's View / 161
  Prebuys / 161

9. LOAN ADMINISTRATION / 162

Selected Problems / 162
  Failure to Complete the Improvements in Conformity
    With the Approved Plans and Specifications / 162
  Open Items After Closing / 163
  Delays Caused By Circumstances Beyond the Control of the Borrower
    or Contractor / 164
  Actual Construction / 164
The Role of the Inspecting Architect
During Loan Administration / 165
The Role of the Lender's Attorney During Loan Administration / 167
Smoothing Out The Mechanics of Construction Loan Advances / 170
  Disbursement Methods / 171
  Prerequisites for Progress Payments / 171
  Responsibilities of the Construction Loan Administrator / 172
  Protecting the Lender Against Mechanics' Liens / 173
  Disbursing Funds Through the Title Insurer / 175
  The Final Advance / 176
Construction Loan Accounting / 177
  Calculation of Interest—Lenders Beware! / 178

10. THE PROBLEM LOAN / 182

Factors to Watch Out For / 182
  Construction Risks / 182
  Monitoring the Loan / 182
Construction Workouts / 183
  Complete Construction / 183
  Participants in the Workout / 184
  Determine Underlying Problems / 184
  Consult With Counsel / 185

xiv CONTENTS

        Defenses / 186
        Feasibility Study / 186
        Options Available to Lender / 187
        Primary Goal / 187
        Control and Ownership of the Project / 188
        Bankruptcy / 189
        Other Factors / 189
        Bonding and Title Companies / 190
        Guarantors / 190
        Third Parties / 190
        Financing During the Workout / 191
        Implementation of the Workout / 191
        Administration of the Workout / 193
        Conclusion / 193
    Bankruptcy and the Problem Loan / 193
        Automatic Stays / 194
        Cramdowns / 195
        Preferences and Fraudulent Transfers / 196
        Recent Court Decisions / 197
    A Case Study: The Workout of a Problem Loan / 198

11. THE PAY-OFF / 205

    Notice / 205
    Role of the Loan Administrator / 206
        Checking Records / 206
        Notify Attorney / 206
        Contact Borrower / 206
        Compile Pay-off Figures / 207
        Confirmation / 208
    Processing Fee / 208
    Assignment to Permanent Mortgagee / 209
    Receipt of Funds / 209

Index / 211

A PRACTICAL GUIDE TO CONSTRUCTION LENDING

1
Introduction

CONSTRUCTION LENDING IN THE 1970s

The course of construction lending in the 1970s exemplified the age-old adage that real estate is a boom-bust industry. There were many reasons for the roller-coaster ride taken by the construction industry in the 1970s, not the least of which was Wall Street's "discovery" in late 1969 of the Real Estate Investment Trust (REIT) as a real estate investment vehicle. In fact, the growth of the REITs in the early 1970s was one of the most significant events affecting the real estate industry in modern times.

The history of the REITs parallels the course of developments in the 1970s but it is uncertain to what extent this popularity of the REITs was a product of the times or itself the cause of the developments. However, if there is to be any understanding of what happened to the real estate industry in the 1970s and the construction lending industry in particular, the rapid growth of REITs and their story must be examined.

The REIT Story

The story started in 1960, when Congress enacted sections 856–858 of the Internal Revenue Code. But it was not until late 1969 that the small investor was made aware of and began looking to the REIT as a vehicle which provided dividends not taxed at the source, as an excellent, although indirect means of diversified participation in real estate. This public demand and the lack of other readily available mortgage money, coupled with a substantial (approved) advisory fee schedule attractive to prospective sponsors such as life insurance companies, banks, brokers, mortgage bankers and real estate companies, led to the proliferation of REITs, which lasted until late 1972.

Since the great majority of emerging REITs were mortgage trusts engaging primarily in construction lending, long-term lending or both, the immediate result was an influx of new capital into the construction industry, creating an abundance of funds available for construction financing and fierce competition among these newly created lenders to put their money to immediate use.

The substantial advisory fees available to REIT sponsors attracted a multitude of sponsors, not all of whom could be classified as "experts" in the real estate field. In addition, since the advisory fee schedule was tied to total assets (at least initially), many REIT advisors concentrated on increasing the assets base by the use of leverage with less than appropriate regard for the quality of the investments the money bought.

Certain blue sky requirements affecting some REITs required two-thirds of the proceeds of an initial public offering of a would-be REIT to be demonstrably capable of being invested in real estate within 60 days of the completion of the offering. This put a premium on haste in addition to the other forces contributing to a composite reckless attitude.

A great number of ill-conceived projects were created to meet and absorb the flood of new money. The availability of funds propelled by the need and desire to invest these funds quickly left little time or inclination for customary lender underwriting considerations to be taken into account. Many construction lenders, particularly the REITs, were no longer looking for good deals, they were looking for almost any deal that would build up the asset base. Deals with "sex appeal"; for example, high interest rates and/or kickers, were the order of the day regardless of the underlying value of the real estate. Consequently, REIT construction loans were made without takeouts and projects were 100% financed. In addition, lender engineering and/or architectural supervision was minimal if not nonexistent and little thought, if any, was given to overbuilding or other factors affecting the viability of the project upon completion of construction.

All of these factors contributed importantly to the boom in the construction of real property improvements, as well as the bust that followed.

The prime rate, to which most REIT and other short-term borrowing was tied, rose to 10%, which was unprecedented at the time, and quickly resulted in the depletion of the interest reserves in specific construction loans.

To make matters worse, many take-out commitments, if they existed at all, were ultimately canceled due to the changed circumstances affecting the projects. REITs and other construction lenders were now seen setting up loss reserves and the so-called era of the "workout" began.

This combination of spiraling cost of money, lack of takeouts and unsophisticated underwriting had a snowballing effect and the unsupervised REITs, more than most other construction lenders, were severely damaged. With REIT dividends now declining and in some instances disappearing, REIT shareholders and debentureholders began to clamor. Shareholder litigation soon followed and the advisory fee schedules, based as they were on a percentage of assets, began to turn on the advisors, precluding them from hiring the personnel needed to work out the abundance of problem loans. To make matters worse, once-friendly bankers began to tighten the screws on credit arrangements, with the overall result that a number of REITs were forced either to de-REIT in order to be in a better position to work out their problems or to file in bankruptcy along with the many developers and contractors who had also overextended themselves during the boom years.

Others

These miseries were by no means limited to REITs. As stated, many developers and contractors also went under, and several of the nation's largest banks, as far as their real estate portfolios were concerned, shared similar fates with the REITs. However, in all fairness to the construction lending industry, and REITs in particular, many of its members survived the mid-1970s with their portfolios pretty much intact. For the most part, with a few notable exceptions, these were all well-managed REITs with life insurance companies and banks as sponsors; or other lenders, developers and contractors who resisted the temptations of easy money and either financed or built quality buildings without unduly overextending their exposure or liabilities.

The Late 1970s

The experiences of the mid-1970s had a cathartic effect upon the construction lending industry. "Bad seeds" were weeded out and mergers and consolidations strengthened otherwise shaky but surviving REIT entities. Inflation helped by raising the inventory value of foreclosed property. Finally, adjustment to the higher prime rate and other inflationary pressures seemed to stablize an industry that was otherwise in disarray.

In particular, the late 1970s and the early 1980s saw an increase in nonresidential construction activity. This increase averaged approximately 4% real annual growth (this compares to approximately 12.1% real negative annual growth for residential construction during the same period) and according to Chicago Title Insurance Company, a leading insurer of property titles (see the March/April 1983 issue of *The Guarantor* published by Chicago Title Insurance Company), 70% of all nonresidential construction activity during this period was located in the Sunbelt, with 43% of all U.S. construction activity taking place in Texas, California and Florida. For example, between 1977 and 1982 Texas experienced real growth at a compounded annual rate of 23.85%. This is illustrated by the following charts* which reflect the average annual rate of change in new nonresidential construction in 1977–82 for the major states and by census regions.

Average Annual Rate of Change in New Nonresidential Construction
(Expressed as a Percentage Increase/Decrease in Constant Dollars)
Major States
1977–82

Rank	U.S. % State	Annual Rate of Increase/Decrease	Total Nonresidential Construction 1977–82 (Billions of Dollars)
	United States	4.0%	$ 200.7
1	Texas	23.8	25.5
2	New York	14.1	6.7
3	Connecticut	14.0	3.0

*Reprinted with permission from the March/April 1983 issue of *The Guarantor* published by Chicago title.

Average Annual Rate of Change (cont.)

Rank	U.S.%State	Annual Rate of Increase/Decrease	Total Nonresidential Construction 1977–82 (Billions of Dollars)
4	Colorado	13.5	4.9
5	Florida	13.4	12.2
6	Arizona	11.2	3.7
7	Missouri	9.4	3.6
8	Washington	8.6	5.3
9	Oklahoma	8.3	3.9
10	Pennsylvania	7.5	5.4
11	Georgia	7.3	4.6
12	New Jersey	5.9	4.5
13	Virginia	5.4	5.3
14	California	5.1	36.5
15	Massachusetts	4.9	4.6
16	Maryland	1.6	3.9
17	North Carolina	−0.6	3.3
18	Minnesota	−1.2	3.9
19	Louisiana	−1.9	3.3
20	Tennessee	−2.5	3.1
21	Ohio	−2.6	8.0
22	Wisconsin	−3.4	2.9
23	Illinois	−7.8	8.4
24	Michigan	−9.7	5.8

Average Annual Rate of Change in New Nonresidential Construction (Expressed as a Percentage Increase/Decrease in Constant Dollars) Components by Census Regions 1977-82

	Total	Office	Industrial	Retail	Additions & Alterations
United States	4.0%	13.6%	−6.2%	−10.5%	28.5%
Northeast	8.1	30.1	−2.3	−9.7	27.7
North Central	−5.5	−2.1	−6.6	−13.6	19.2
South	8.8	24.1	−5.2	−4.2	29.9
West	4.6	18.6	−3.4	−9.3	23.8

Summary

In perspective, the commercial construction lending industry started off the 1970s in a boom cycle. This was followed by a bust period in the mid 1970s, which in turn was followed by steady growth and at least a miniboom in certain areas (e.g., new office construction) in the late 1970s and continuing into the early 1980s. This miniboom has itself been a factor in the current slowdown of new commercial construction which will be described in more detail in the next selection.

CONSTRUCTION LENDING TODAY

It is too early to tell whether today's construction lending community has mastered the lessons to be learned from the 1970s. Continued inflation, sky-high interest rates and the changing nature of the permanent take-out commitment until quite recently have forced construction lenders to take a closer look at their investments. Should interest rates continue to recede and investment capital become more available, it will be interesting to see if today's underwriting standards reflect a wiser lending community than was previously the case, or are merely the natural outcome of tight money.

Criteria

In any event, the criteria utilized today by construction lenders to underwrite and monitor their loans are certainly different from those used in the 1970s. No longer do we see commitments for construction financing issued on the basis of ideas alone. Construction lenders now almost uniformly insist upon appraisals and feasibility studies of the project, prior approval of plans and specifications, personal guarantees and even bonding of the general contractor or major subcontractors before agreeing to advance any funds. In addition, construction loans without take-out commitments are now the exception rather than the rule, and when made will almost always be restricted to borrowers who are strong financially with proven track records, for the construction of projects which upon completion will make excellent equity investments.

Take-out Commitment

Perhaps the most significant real estate development today has been the change in the form and nature of the permanent take-out commitment. The new forms of takeout that have replaced the conventional mortgage seem to be taking any one of four basic forms, each of which contains its own variations and in some instances offers challenges to the construction lender. They are: (1) interest rate adjusted mortgages; (2) mortgages with additional interest provisions; (3) land purchase leasebacks; and (4) partnership interests including mortgage/equity combinations. In addition, it is becoming more and more prevalent for permanent lenders to substitute 100% equity purchases in the form of prebuys in place of conventional mortgages. However, with the recent drop in interest rates and the inflationary index, as well as the availability of additional investment capital, we are once again seeing fixed rate mortgages, albeit for much shorter terms (5-12 years) than had previously prevailed, although these mortgages are still not being issued as forward commitments prior to the commencement of construction.

Source of Financing

Accompanying this change in the form of takeout has been a shift in the source of both construction and long-term financing. According to *The Mortgage and Real Estate Executives Report* (Vol. 14 No. 17), in 1973, 74% of construction financing came from commercial banks, savings associations and savings banks. This percentage rose to 84% in 1980, with commercial banks accounting for seven-eighths of the total. The increased activity of commercial banks in the construction lending field is attributable to the reduced role of real estate investment trusts and the fact that commercial banks are best suited to make construction loans. They can do everything other institutional lenders can do plus make commercial loans, issue letters of credit, control disbursement of loan funds by monitoring checks and provide a wide range of other services that others cannot provide.

On the long-term financing side, banks and savings associations accounted for 67% of long-term originations in 1973 but only 50% in

1980. This decline traces its origins to the shift from long-term debt financing to equity participations which life insurance companies and mortgage banking companies seem best suited to make. In addition, the availability of equity positions has attracted a massive influx of foreign capital looking for safety and stability more than yields. Most of this money has come from West Germany, other countries of Western Europe and Canada; however, with the recent strengthening of the dollar relative to European currencies, the pace of this foreign investment has declined.

Another new entry into the field of real estate financing has been the pension funds as a group. Commingled and separate real estate accounts designed as vehicles for investing pension fund assets in real estate have been cropping up everywhere. Unfortunately, these accounts for the most part have not attracted the kinds of dollars originally anticipated. Nonetheless, the present and anticipated dollar volume of pension funds (in the trillions of dollars by the year 2000) make this the largest potential source of capital available for real estate development.

Industrial Development Bond Financing

Until 1983, the scarcity of traditional sources of financing and sky-high interest rates led both large and small developers to seek other methods of financing their projects. These factors, combined with changes in the tax laws and a more liberal interpretation of state regulations have in turn led to the emergence of tax-free industrial development bonds (IDBs) as a source of below-market construction and long-term financing. The drop in interest rates in 1983–84 and more readily available capital have not served as yet to significantly diminish the popularity of the IDBs.

IDBs are basically revenue bonds issued by states or local municipal agencies, with the proceeds being used for development of private projects. The developer markets the bonds and is the source of their credit rating, but since the bonds are actually issued by the government agency, the income is tax free to the investors. Historically, these bonds were used almost exclusively for industrial development, particularly in the South. They may now be used in a substantial number of jurisdictions to finance both industrial and commercial projects.

Provided certain requirements are adhered to, up to $10 million may be raised in a single municipality, thus permitting 100% financing of a project in addition to interest rate payments of 3-4% lower than those of corporate bonds. Other benefits derived from the use of IDBs include the possible exemption from sales taxes, use and ad valorum taxes and assistance from the municipality with the costs of roads, utilities and site preparation.

Although the benefits to be derived from the use of IDBs are substantial and their use has accelerated dramatically over the years, problems relating to adherence with capital expenditure requirements, obtaining the approval of the government agency issuing the bonds and actually marketing the bonds have limited their usefulness. In addition, the Congress and the Internal Revenue Service (IRS) now are looking into abuses of the issuance of IDBs. It is quite possible that in the near future, additional laws and regulations will further restrict their use.

New Activity

Commercial construction activity proceeded at a much slower pace in 1983 than it had over the preceding five years. This was generally true of all areas of nonresidential construction (except for additions and alterations), as illustrated by the following charts.*

Components of Nonresidential Construction in Millions of Dollars

	1980	1981	PERCENT CHANGE (1980-81)	1982	PERCENT CHANGE (1981-82)
Total U.S.	36,023	42,145	+17	38,300	−9
Commercial (Office)	8,658	13,211	+53	9,200	−30
Industrial	5,450	5,450	*	4,800	−12
Retail Stores	5,361	4,959	−7	4,200	−15
Additions and Alterations	9,934	11,528	+16	13,100	+14
All Other	6,620	6,997	+6	7,000	*

*Reprinted with permission from the March/April 1983 issue of *Guarantor* published by Chicago Title.

Nonresidential Construction in Millions of Dollars by Census Regions

	1980	1981	Percent Change (1980-81)	1982	Percent Change (1981-82)
Total U.S.	36,023	42,145	+17	38,300	-9
Northeast	4,484	5,951	+33	5,200	-13
North Central	7,526	7,185	-5	6,500	-10
South	12,836	16,293	+27	15,000	-8
West	11,177	12,716	+14	11,600	-9

The recent sustained recession and boom in energy and in office construction, has led to increased vacancy levels in both office and industrial space. According to The Office Network, as reported in the February 1983 issue of Dun's *Business Month* (pages 80-85), the national vacancy rate has risen to 7.5% and the recent boom cities of Chicago, Denver, Dallas and Houston are reporting high vacancy levels. Denver in particular has a vacancy level of 15.8%, and even Washington, D.C., perhaps the best office market in the country, has seen its vacancy level of 0.3% in 1980-81 rise to 2.7% by 1983-84. The result has been a severe dropoff in construction activity throughout most areas of the country which is only now starting to pickup with the economy once again expanding.

By Type of Construction. New commercial construction activity for 1984 by type of construction should continue as follows:

Office Buildings. Since most U.S. cities have more office space than can be absorbed, commercial office construction should remain flat and may even face sharp reductions in certain areas, with the possible exception of well-located and established office-oriented parks in the nation's growth centers. It is estimated that in many metropolitan areas it will take between two to five years to absorb the excess supply of office space, even assuming that demand rises to prerecession levels.

Industrial Space. This type of space is typically "built to suit." Consequently, the problems now facing industrial real estate do not involve oversupply, but rather are due to changing markets, obsolete facilities and recessionary conditions. The trend away from heavy manufacturing toward the information and processing industries has on the one hand created large amounts of obsolete space (particularly in the older industrial cities), and on the other hand a need for new research and development (R&D) facilities. As the economic recovery picks up steam, an upturn in new industrial starts should follow fairly quickly, with particular emphasis on R&D facilities and renovation of existing "obsolete space" for adaptive reuse.

Retail Space. The continued trend toward smaller stores has reduced overall space demand and this situation will probably continue until the mid 1980s. High unemployment, changes in personal buying patterns (particularly the result of the aging of the population) and some overbuilding of shopping centers, among other factors, do not augur well for new shopping center starts in 1984. Most new construction activity is likely to be limited to modernization of existing centers.

Hospitality Facilities. The hotel industry's fortunes are closely tied to the economy. If the economic recovery is sustained and long lasting, both business and vacation travel should increase. In such event, new construction will probably be centered around budget motels and luxury hotels as opposed to the middle-level variety. (See *The Mortgage and Real Estate Executives Report,* Vol. 15, No. 22, January 15, 1983.)

Residential Properties. Years of poor maintenance and rising rents have spurred renewed investor interests in rental construction which should surge throughout 1984 in all areas of the country and especially in the South which has seen the highest increase in population.

Alterations and Additions. The only form of nonresidential construction that had not experienced a decline in activity in 1982–83 had been alterations and additions. This trend is expected to continue, with most of the alterations taking place in the older North Central and Northeast regions and with the rapidly growing Sunbelt experiencing most of the additions to existing facilities.

Both developments in the economy and changes in the tax laws have contributed to this growth. Inflated construction costs and high interest rates oftentimes make it more economical to rehabilitate existing older buildings (particularly in the North Central and Northeast regions) than erect new ones. The Economic Tax Recovery Act of 1981 (ERTA), notwithstanding certain modifications contained in the Tax Equity and Fiscal Responsibility Act of 1982, also gave a boost to reconstruction projects by replacing the existing 10% investment tax credit with a more favorable three-tier 15% tax credit for structures 30 years old, 20% for structures 40 years old and 25% for certified historical structures. The intent of Congress, which was to discourage relocation of businesses from older, economically distressed communities to new locations, seems to be working.

By Region. New commercial construction activity for 1984 by region should continue as follows:

Midwest. The Midwest was and still is particularly hard hit by the recent recession and there is comparatively little new development going on. Overbuilding of office space in major cities has led to increased selectivity with a trend toward high-tech building in planned unit development parks containing office and R&D facilities. In addition, the fact that raw land for construction is scarce in good locations is putting an additional damper on new construction.

West. Development in the West, which has until very recently been fairly steady (with that part of the West located in the Sunbelt, i.e., Southern California, having the most activity), is also experiencing a slow-down due to higher vacancy rates. Denver in particular has been hard hit by overbuilt conditions, as has Seattle. However, demand for R&D space is still quite strong, with Los Angeles, San Diego, San Jose and even Denver reporting vigorous activity in this area.

Southwest. A slackening of demand has even been felt in this area that was once thought of as recession-proof. Office space built for the burgeoning oil business and for companies relocating to the Sunbelt has remained vacant due to the current pinch being felt by the oil-related industries, and companies deciding to sit tightly until the general economy improves. Houston, for example, went from a 4% vacancy rate in 1979 to an 11.4% vacancy rate in 1982.

Southeast. Except for an increase in high-tech companies leasing space, this region is suffering from the same overbuilt conditions as the rest of the country, with the South Florida area suffering the least.

Northeast. For many years now, this region has been experiencing a decline of manufacturing facilities caused by companies relocating to the Sunbelt. However, the region is still growing due to an increase in government contracts and the high-technology industry, which continues to bring new jobs and the need for more office and industrial parks, particularly in New England and specifically around the Boston area. In addition, there has been some local expansion of distribution and service centers and light manufacturing, giving cause for new construction or renovation of existing buildings and inner city development. In some locations, most notably New York, this expansion has been extensive, and has helped to make up for years of neglect.

Summary

Until quite recently, economic conditions dried up traditional sources of financing due to a shift in financing sources and developers have been forced to seek creative methods of financing as a means of survival. Notwithstanding the 1983–84 decline in interest rates and comparative abundance of investment capital, previous overbuilding combined with a sustained recession has led to high vacancy rates in offices and industrial space throughout the nation. Except in a few special areas, the bulk of new construction, when it has taken place, has been very selective and geared toward high-technology office and industrial parks and to rehabilitation of existing space. New apartment projects are more popular forms of investments, but very few new hotels are being constructed, except possibly in a few markets such as New York that have experienced an acute shortage of hotel space. In addition, the large regional shopping centers have given way to neighborhood and specialty type shopping centers with new construction here being limited as well.

UPDATE 1984

The economic recovery of 1983 resulted in an absorption of existing vacancies at a much greater pace than originally forecast. John

Pfister, Vice President and Market Research Manager of Chicago Title and Trust Co., reported in the March/April 1984 issue of *The Guarantor* that nonresidential construction was up 6.6 percent in 1983 over 1982 and that a gain of 10.4 percent over 1983 totals was projected for 1984. In 1984, new construction of retail stores should enjoy the largest percentage gain over the prior year of any category, and additions and alterations, including rehab structures and improvements to existing buildings, should account for the greatest dollar volume. Moreover, approximately 40 percent of the new construction is expected to take place in the southern states, although, on a state-by-state basis, California should lead the nation in dollar volume, followed by Texas, Florida, Illinois, and New York.

In a comparison of metropolitan areas, Los Angeles is targeted for the highest dollar volume of activity, followed by Dallas/Ft. Worth, Houston, San Francisco, and Chicago. From this category, San Francisco should lead the nation in new office construction; San Jose, California, should be the leader in new industrial construction; Chicago should lead in the additions and alterations category; and Dallas/Ft. Worth should lead in retail store construction. The foregoing is illustrated by the following charts.*

U.S. Nonresidential Construction by Type of Building
1982–1984
(in Millions of Dollars)

	1982	1983	1984	PERCENT CHANGE 1984/83
TOTAL	$48,677	$51,900	$57,300	+ 10.4
Industrial	6,075	5,540	5,980	+ 8.0
Office	12,938	12,820	13,960	+ 8.9
Stores	5,531	6,970	7,960	+ 14.2
Additions and Alterations	13,895	16,050	17,600	+ 9.7
Other	10,238	10,520	11,800	+ 12.4

*Reprinted with permission from the March/April 1984 issue of *The Guarantor*, published by Chicago Title and Trust Co.

U.S. Nonresidential Construction by Region
1982-1984
(in Millions of Dollars)

	1982	1983	1984	Percent Change 2984/83
TOTAL	$48,676	$51,900	$57,300	+ 10.4
Northeast	7,241	6,880	7,780	+ 13.1
North Central	8,823	9,860	10,520	+ 6.7
South	19,366	20,810	23,270	+ 11.8
West	13,246	14,350	15,730	+ 9.6

U.S. Nonresidential Construction
Top Ten States
1982-1984
(in Millions of Dollars)

	1982	1983	1984	Percent Change 1984/83
1. California	$7,497	$8,180	$9,150	+ 11.9
2. Texas	6,878	6,775	6,960	+ 2.7
3. Florida	3,258	4,050	4,650	+ 14.9
4. Illinois	1,873	2,100	2,330	+ 11.2
5. New York	2,151	1,710	1,970	+ 15.2
6. Ohio	1,534	1,840	1,880	+ 2.2
7. Pennsylvania	1,560	1,465	1,625	+ 10.9
8. Virginia	1,153	1,380	1,550	+ 12.3
9. New Jersey	1,423	1,270	1,395	+ 9.8
10. Washington	1,186	1,200	1,360	+ 13.3

U.S. Nonresidential Construction by SMSA*
1982-1984 (in Millions of dollars)

SMSA	1982	1983	1984	Percent Change 1984/83
1. Los Angeles, CA	$2,355	$2,378	$2,560	+ 7.7
2. Dallas/Fort Worth, TX	2,050	2,190	2,060	− 5.9
3. Houston, TX	2,752	2,040	2,050	+ 0.5
4. San Francisco, CA	1,469	1,780	2,030	+ 14.0

U.S. Nonresidential Construction by SMSA* (cont.)

SMSA	1982	1983	1984	PERCENT CHANGE 1984/83
5. Chicago, IL	1,494	1,470	1,640	+ 11.4
6. Washington, DC	1,083	1,160	1,310	+ 12.9
7. New York City, NY	1,261	840	1,170	+ 39.3
8. Atlanta, GA	660	885	840	− 5.1
9. San Jose, CA	570	860	830	− 3.5
10. St. Petersburg/Tampa, FL	499	670	800	+ 19.4
11. Denver, CO	852	755	730	− 3.3
12. Philadelphia, PA	632	678	725	+ 6.9
13. Detroit, MI	551	612	705	+ 15.2
14. Minneapolis/St. Paul, MN	712	630	695	+ 10.3
15. Anaheim/Santa Ana, CA	620	600	675	+ 12.5
16. San Diego, CA	521	610	660	+ 8.2
17. Phoenix, AZ	518	560	655	+ 17.0
18. Boston, MA	570	555	650	+ 17.1
19. Miami, FL	470	575	640	+ 11.7
20. Seattle, WA	760	555	610	+ 9.9
21. Riverside/San Bernardino, CA	433	501	570	+ 13.8
22. St. Louis, MO	591	495	565	+ 14.1
23. Baltimore, MD	515	505	555	+ 9.9
24. Orlando, FL	433	490	550	+ 12.2
25. Newark, NJ	499	446	498	+ 11.7
26. Sacramento, CA	322	435	495	+ 13.8
27. Austin, TX	328	415	490	+ 18.1
28. Pittsburgh, PA	326	395	440	+ 11.4
29. Cleveland, OH	317	551	430	− 22.0
30. Fort Lauderdale, FL	348	372	420	+ 12.9
31. New Orleans, LA	503	475	410	− 13.7
32. San Antonio, TX	338	355	410	+ 15.5
33. West Palm Beach, FL	342	322	370	+ 14.9
34. Kansas City, MO	252	310	350	+ 12.9
35. Las Vegas, NV	170	360	345	− 4.2
36. Indianapolis, IN	218	355	325	− 8.5
37. Cincinnati, OH	210	340	315	− 7.4
38. Portland, OR	344	252	305	+ 21.0
39. Oklahoma City, OK	337	278	300	+ 7.9
40. Memphis, TN	233	257	290	+ 12.8
41. Columbus, OH	360	225	285	+ 26.7
42. Salt Lake City, UT	297	232	285	+ 22.8
43. Nashville, TN	260	242	275	+ 13.6
44. Milwaukee, WI	172	255	270	+ 5.9
45. Honolulu, HA	208	148	170	+ 14.9
46. Buffalo, NY	167	85	110	+ 29.4

*Standard Metropolitan Statistical Area

CONSTRUCTION LENDING TOMORROW

It is difficult to predict with any degree of certainty, the amount, place and type of new development that will be prevalent in the future. Certainly, interest rates, inflation, continued decentralization, migration, population and household profiles and energy will all be factors. The slowed pace of construction in 1983, notwithstanding the generally overbuilt conditions, should continue to spur new development. In light of this and other factors that will be examined, most experts feel that the demand for real estate over the next five years will be strong although focused on specific areas.

Interest Rates

Sustained high interest rates have served to slow the rate of real estate development. These rates are declining but they are still high by historical standards. However, as developers continue to adjust to high rates and find creative means to finance their projects, the pace of new development should increase, barring other factors, even if interest rates remain at current levels or even increase slightly. The outlook though is for rates to continue to drop, notwithstanding periodic fluctuations upward, which can only serve to spur new construction. The pressure on the Federal Reserve Bank to further lower rates and on the Congress to come to grips with the budgetary process have been tremendous and should continue.

Inflation

Real estate has proven over the years to be an excellent hedge against inflation. Significant strides have been taken to reduce previously high levels of inflation, although it is still to early to say whether inflation is really firmly under control or just temporarily lowered. The problem is just too ingrained in the economy and is not subject to quick solution. The result is that real estate will continue in demand as an inflationary hedge placing emphasis on construction of office buildings and warehouses which are subject to short-term leases that can be adjusted upward along with the inflation rate. Conversely, regional shopping centers with traditional long-term leases will not be in vogue.

Decentralization

Over the years our economy has also changed from one heavily reliant upon capital-intensive industries to knowledge industries. This shift is expected to continue with the result that great concentrations of labor will no longer be mandatory in central locations. Thus, the movement away from the major metropolitan areas to so-called "second-tier" cities will intensify. Property values in the second-tier cities should outpace those in the major metropolitan areas and the second-tier cities should receive an increased percentage of investment capital for real estate development. This is not to say that real estate development in the major metropolitan areas will die. On the contrary, increased energy costs will still make central city locations attractive and recent inner city renovation has reversed social and economic blight in many cities, lessening the desire of the populace for a change in life-style to the smaller localities.

Migration

Migration from the Northeast and Midwest to the Southwest and West is expected to continue due primarily to the energy related industries being located in the Southwest and West and people's desire for a change in life-style. This will continue the trend of greater real estate development in the Southwest and West.

Population and Household Profiles

In the years to come, we will see an increased percentage of elderly comprising our population. This will create a demand for new nursing homes and retirement facilities to be developed. In addition, births are once again on the rise which should create a demand for new housing. Fertility patterns are dramatically different in different regions and thus the effect of the births will vary across the nation. In any event, since apartment rentals cannot be increased as readily as those for office buildings or warehouses, as long as inflation continues the demand for new housing will contrast with the financial community's reluctance to place money into the housing market. Perhaps the solution to the housing problem will be an influx of investment capital into the multifamily condominium market as opposed to the traditional high-rise apartment "for rent" buildings.

Energy

Energy costs will, as indicated, continue to play a role in real estate development. Increased costs will serve somewhat to counteract the move to second-tier cities and foster growth in central locations. Energy-conserving construction techniques will also play a part in the type of building materials and the architectural design of the future.

Other Factors

The current emphasis on savings as opposed to consumption should also be a factor in future real estate development and will have an adverse impact on the development of regional shopping centers which are dependent upon consumer spending. Possible changes in the tax laws may also have a material impact on real estate development. Should the suggested flat tax ever be enacted and deductions for depreciation and interest payments eliminated, there will be a decrease in property values not seen since the Depression. Real estate has always traded on a lower dollar-to-dollar yield than other forms of investment due primarily to the significant tax benefits derived from owning real estate. Should these tax benefits be eliminated or significantly reduced, investors will be requiring a greater return for their money and assuming the income remains constant, this can only be accomplished by lowering the overall price of the property.

Growth Patterns

According to a study prepared by the MIT and Harvard Joint Center for Urban Studies entitled "Regional Diversity: Growth in the United States," as reported in *The Mortgage and Real Estate Executives Report* (Vol. 14, No. 19, December 1, 1981), there are four groups of regions in the United States which will have varying growth patterns over the next 10 years. The fast growth regions will be in the Sunbelt and Mountain States and extend basically from Kentucky in the east to New Mexico in the west. Those regions which will experience decelerating growth are comprised of the South Atlantic region (the Carolinas, Florida and Georgia in particular) and the Pacific region (notably California). The reasons given for the slowdown in growth for the Atlantic region are threefold; that is, retirees will be no longer be converging on Florida alone; wages are rising thereby diminishing the competitive edge of industry; and the fertility rate of young adults is dropping sharply. In the Pacific region, excess labor supply, high housing prices, limited wear and sensitivity to economic slowdowns, tempered by a high fertility rate should serve to reduce immigration rates.

New England and West North Central (Minnesota, Iowa, Missouri, the Dakotas, Nebraska and Kansas) are described in the study as the resurgent growth regions due primarily to historic low wage levels which attract industry and an ample supply of affordable rural areas to live in which attract people. The no-growth regions include the East North Central and Mid-Atlantic regions, including New York, New Jersey, Pennsylvania, Ohio, Michigan, Illinois and Wisconsin. These states are likely to lose population and show no discernible economic growth at all.

The conclusion of the Joint Center study was that the nation will face only modest growth in the years to come, with rural and metropolitan areas competing for industry, people and public services. The winners will experience the greatest rise in real estate values. In addition, the urban areas that anticipate rapid growth will have to allocate capital to serve children (schools), young adults (housing, water, sewerage, transit, roads), and the elderly (public housing, special services). These allocations will have a direct effect upon the types and profitability of real estate development in the areas affected.

Summary

Norcross "Pete" Teel, Jr., President of MONY Mortgage Investors, a REIT actively engaged in construction lending and Vice President in charge of real estate operations at The Mutual Life Insurance Company of New York, recently summarized in an interview the outlook for real estate development in the 1980s. He stated that

> Office space will continue to be developed to house the white-collar workers necessary for the country's growing service economy. The pace of

development will be restrained until the surplus of space constructed in the early eighties is absorbed. Office space in the eighties will differ in several aspects from that of prior years as a result of the lofty rental rates required by current construction and capital costs. Square footage provided per worker will be reduced, more sites heretofore considered secondary will be utilized, and there will be an increased use of one- and two-story space which can be constructed at a lower cost than buildings with more stories. Retail development will focus on stores for discount operations and the rehabilitation and upgrading of existing centers. The collapse of Grant's and Woolco's does not mean discounting is dead. Major retailers will move to fill this void although in locations removed from their regular operations. Housing should be strong for all types—single-family detached, condominiums and rental apartments. The demographics indicate substantial pent-up demand which sooner or later is to be transferred into housing starts.

2
Loan Underwriting

THE APPLICATION PROCESS

The Lender's Staff

Commercial construction lending is generally considered to be the most exposed form of real estate financing, balancing the highest risks with the highest rewards. In order for a lender to be successful in this field, it must commit itself entirely, acquiring a dedicated staff of competent professionals with the ability to see the loan through the application process to the final payoff. This staff of key personnel should include mortgage loan underwriters capable of analyzing and accepting risk; loan administrators with the ability to handle all aspects of the loan short of underwriting and negotiations; operations people with specific expertise in such areas as leasing and hazard insurance, etc.; an appraisal staff or loan officers with appraisal background capable of preparing in-house appraisals or analyzing outside appraisals; architects and/or engineers to review cost estimates, plans, specifications and contracts and to make progress inspections or review and approve the progress inspections made by outside professionals; and attorneys with extensive real estate experience.

Lending Policy

Assuming the lender has access to the professionals referred to in the preceding paragraph, it should be in a position to screen applications for construction loans. However, in doing so lenders either have or should have a basic lending policy which they generally adhere to in approving loans. Preferably, this policy will call for establishing ongoing relationships with developers and take-out lenders among others and result in a balanced loan portfolio. Policy decisions may permit loans only on certain types of properties and in certain localities, set upper and lower dollar limits on the loans, restrict loans to proven developers with good track records and minimum net worths and require take-out financing with institutions that have established records of acceptable performance.

On a philosophical basis, lenders will either restrict their loans to good real estate deals, good credit deals or a combination of both.

Initial Screening Process

The loan application submitted to the lender will either come directly from the developer, particularly if the lender and developer have done business in the past or, more commonly, through a broker or correspondent. The application should set forth the details of the proposed construction; for example, type, size and location of the building, the proposed loan terms, the track record of the developer, the net worth of the intended borrower and guarantors and the existence of any preleasing (letters of intent) and projected rental for the building. It should also be accompanied by a preliminary cost breakdown; detailed plans and specifications (sufficient to apply for a building permit); a copy of the take-out commitment, if any; and a pro forma income and expense statement. Should this information indicate a proposed project not within the lender's policy guidelines, barring special circumstances, the loan application should be declined immediately. It will do the lender's reputation no good and may severely harm the developer if a lender delays responding to a loan application the lender knows will not be accepted. On the other hand, should the promise of a loan exist, the lender will most likely call for additional information from the developer and the real loan underwriting process will begin.

THE UNDERWRITING PROCESS

Economic Viability of the Project

The first step in the underwriting process is to determine the economic viability of the project. To accomplish this, the lender should review the preliminary plans and specifications, cost breakdown, pro forma income and expense statements, financial statements of the borrower and guarantors and a feasibility study. Assuming there is a long-term mortgage to be placed on the property, the construction lender should satisfy itself that there will be sufficient income from the property adequately to cover the debt service of the long-term mortgage and provide a reasonable return to the owner. Generally, debt service coverage of between 1.20–1.25 to 1 is acceptable. However, the true litmus test is for the construction lender to be willing to own the project at completion for the amount of its loan.

Location. It is common to hear that the three most important factors in determining the success of real estate are location, location and location. This is certainly true to an extent; however, other factors such as the nature and size of the proposed project in relation to the needs of the locality, supply and demand factors, inventory and absorption rates, the parking ratios for the project and its salability upon completion will all be factors in determining value. Comparables in the area should also be looked at and comparisons made within other units in the area to determine reasonableness. A site inspection of the property should reflect an area that is stable or improving and discussions with other lenders, leasing agents, realtors, appraisers and mortgage bankers should justify the pro forma income and expense projections and tend to confirm the value of the property upon completion.

Income. The actual value and quality of the income projected for the project must be reviewed very carefully by the lender. In these times of low inflation, applicants may be projecting higher space rentals upon completion than are justified given the oversupply of space in most areas. It is incumbent upon the lender to analyze the applicant's projections to determine if they are reasonable based upon current supply and demand factors as well as those projected for the time when the property will be completed.

When the project is preleased, the quality of the income becomes the prevalent factor to be considered. A long-term net lease from a credit tenant is obviously of more value to the project than short-term leases to local or regional tenants. To begin with, there is a much greater likelihood that the credit tenant will still be around when the project is completed. At this point, the viability of the project will be pretty much assured since the owners will have a steady income stream from which to pay the debt service on the long-term loan.

Expenses. The expenses projected must also be reviewed very carefully by the lender. Comparables must be checked and once again, inquiries should be made of other lenders, leasing agents and managers, etc., to ascertain their experience in the locality with regard to expense of operations. Projected expenses for the time of completion should be estimated as was done with projected income.

Capitalization Rate. Once the projected income for the project and the expenses reasonably required to carry the project have been determined, the lender should be in a position to set the capitalization rate and arrive at a value. This is an all-important procedure, with capitalization being defined by Byrl N. Boyce, Ph.D., *Real Estate Appraisal Terminology* (1975) as "The process of converting into present value (or obtaining the present worth of) a series of anticipated periodic installments of net income. In real estate appraising, it usually takes the form of discounting." Basically, this involves discounting future incomes into present value.

Project Costs

The next step in the underwriting process is a determination by the lender that there are sufficient funds available, either from the loan or outside sources, to complete the project. This determination is critically important in order to safeguard the lender from being left with an incomplete building after all of the loan proceeds have been exhausted. Thus, a prudent lender will not close its loan unless these funds exist, including a reasonable contingency for both hard and soft costs, with any necessary funds in excess of the loan proceeds either going into the project before the lender disburses its funds, or being deposited with the lender in the form of a certificate of deposit or letter of credit. However, as an exception in the case of an extremely creditworthy applicant, some requisite equity money may be permitted to be infused into the project after the construction loan is closed, provided the lender is assured these funds will be available on a timely basis.

To determine whether there exist sufficient funds to complete the project, the lender must first review the applicant's cost breakdown to insure that all items of construction expense are included. This procedure will usually be performed by the architect/engineer and is discussed in more detail later on. However, it should be pointed out that particular care needs to be taken in reviewing estimated costs (especially where there is no construction contract), development or "soft" costs and the interest expense included within the definition of soft costs during the construction period. This latter determination will usually be done by the lender's loan underwriter and not the architect/engineer.

Take-Out Financing

The final step in the loan underwriting process is to insure that the conditions of any permanent take-out financing will be satisfied upon completion of the construction so that upon such completion, the provider of take-out funds will not be in a position once again to underwrite its transaction. This will entail funding only up to the floor amount of the takeout and making arrangements, approved by all parties, for gap financing if necessary. All take-out requirements that reasonably can be satisfied prior to disbursement of the construction loan should be resolved and a buy-sell or tripartite agreement reflecting this and the parties' several rights executed by all three concerned parties.

The provisions of the takeout which ordinarily may be satisfied prior to a construction loan closing include: (1) approval of the title insurance and hazard insurance coverage; (2) satisfaction of environmental requirements and approval of plans and specifications from all appropriate governmental agencies subject to the issuance of a final certificate of occupancy; (3) approval of the soil engineer's report; (4) written evidence that all necessary utilities will be available to the project in the capacity needed; (5) approval of credit reports and the financial condition of the borrower or guarantors; (6) possible deletion of any "adverse change" provisions; (7) approval of the appraisal; (8) inclusion of a force majeure clause in the take-out commitment; (9) coordination of periodic inspections during construction; (10) approval of existing leases and arranging for the prompt approval of future leases; (11) payment of any take-out commitment fees; (12) approval of the form of opinion letters required; (13) definition of what approvals are needed to evidence completion of construction and (14) entering into the buy–sell or tripartite agreement.

Risk Factor

Notwithstanding the prior approval by the provider of permanent financing to all of the foregoing, the risk of completing construction and obtaining a final certificate of occupancy remains with the construction lender. However, this risk can be minimized by the construction lender itself reviewing and approving the plans and specifications, cost breakdowns, engineer's report on soil conditions, the building permit, the environmental impact report, all construction contracts and establishing and adhering to a strict disbursement and inspection procedure. Toward this end, the construction lender should permit "fast track" construction only when there is a strong general contractor who is willing to enter into a guaranteed maximum or turnkey contract which includes a provision deferring collection of any cost overruns from the borrower until the construction loan has been paid in full. In addition, should the construction lender close its loan on the basis of only a demolition or foundation permit being issued as opposed to a building permit allowing full completion of the proposed improvements, it must be first assured that the issuance of the final building permit will be a routine matter after certain specified requirements of the municipality have been satisfied.

CREDIT ANALYSIS

An analysis of the financial capability of the borrower to complete the project is an integral part of any underwriting process. (This is particularly true of banks, as opposed to REITS, which put a premium on their continuing relationship with and creditworthiness of the borrower.) For no matter how high the underlying value of the real estate may be, if the borrower runs into financial difficulties and is unable to pay its debts when due, the successful completion of the project will be jeopardized. Conversely, if the real estate turns sour and/or cost overruns arise, the lender will be looking to the borrower to bail out the project.

Net Worth Requirements

For these reasons and several others, it becomes a basic criterion for loan approval, that the borrower and any guarantors have an established aggregate net worth exceeding certain minimum levels set by the lender. These levels will vary from transaction to transaction, depending upon the size and nature of the deal; the past record of the developer; the existence of guaranteed price contracts and preleasing and among numerous other factors, the liquidity of the borrower's assets and the quality of his net worth and ability to raise additional funds if needed. In this regard, lenders generally work under the assumption that they can never be too secure.

Verification of Net Worth

To verify the net worth of the borrower and guarantors, lenders should receive audited financial statements and income and expense statements on the individuals and if corporations are involved, income and expense statements, balance sheets and annual reports. The lender's personnel should be capable of reading and interpreting this material. Surprisingly, some lenders are incapable of doing this and many borrowers and guarantors who are purported to have high net worths at the time of loan approval, turn out to be near insolvency when they are called upon to infuse additional capital into the project.

How to Read a Financial Report

One of the basic credit skills that every loan underwriter should have is the ability to read a financial report. Any underwriter who asserts that such reports are "over my head" should be in a different profession.

Auditor's Report.   Generally, lenders require that the financial statements submitted by developers be audited by a certified public accountant. However, since audited statements are costly and time consuming to prepare, lenders sometimes accept lower-cost reviews or compilations, or even a statement signed by a principal of the developer, in lieu of a full-scale audit. Depending upon the amount of the loan, other debts of the developer and the developer's record, lenders will be more inclined to accept unaudited statements under circumstances where the loan is well secured; the developer has a longstanding relationship with the lender; the developer has made profitable deals and has a "good" capital structure and owns a sizable amount of liquid assets and attractive real estate.

The Financial Report. The figures contained in the financial report tell the real story of the borrower; and although no story is ever fully complete since it is only valid as of the date of the report and cannot foretell the consequences of all future events, it will tell you the borrower's present strength and to what extent the borrower can weather future crisis.

Balance Sheet. This is an important source of figures. It reflects the financial strength of the borrower by showing what it owns and owes on a certain date. The difference between current assets and current liabilities constitutes net working capital and is the key figure for the underwriter to focus upon. This will tell the underwriter whether the borrower will be in a position to make up for possible shortages in cash flow. It may also reflect, when compared with prior reports, the borrower's ability to maintain existing growth patterns. These are very important considerations to a construction lender who is basically involved with the borrower and has an exposure only over the period it takes to construct the building.

Income Statement. This is another important source of figures. It tells how the borrower performed in the current year in comparison to the previous years. The trap that many underwriters fall into is to look just at the bottom line (net earnings) and stop there. Net earnings can be affected by the sale of an asset, a change in accounting methods or other matters that may increase current earnings but depress future earnings. The underwriter's review of the income statement is not finished until he ascertains how the net income came about and how it may come about next year. The key here is recurring earnings as opposed to extraordinary one-time events.

Comparisons. No review of a financial report is completed until comparisons are made with prior years' reports or with the reports of similar developers. The comparisons will tell if management is on top of its job.

Conclusion

A credit analysis does not start nor stop with a review of the financial report. In order to know all you can about an individual or company, a little homework needs to be done. Business press reports may be available and the company or individual's word-of-mouth reputation as to doing business and fulfilling commitments can be extremely helpful. Finally, the ability of the borrower to complete the project will be affected by current events and thus it becomes incumbent upon the underwriter to be conversant with what's going on in business, economics and politics, locally, nationally and around the world.

THE ROLE OF THE CONSTRUCTION ARCHITECT/ENGINEER IN THE LOAN UNDERWRITING PROCESS

An integral part of any loan underwriting process involves the review by the lender of the project's cost estimates and the proposed plans and specifications. Before issuing its commitment for construction financing, the lender should be satisfied that the project as contemplated is structurally sound and well designed and that the proposed costs are realistic. An analysis of these factors is usually done by the lender's own in-house personnel or by an independent engineering or architectural firm. However, lenders are strongly advised to resist the use of their own personnel for such purposes unless they have on staff a capable engineer or architect. The decisions to be made here are engineer oriented, and financially oriented personnel generally do not have the necessary expertise to perform the functions required. There is a dearth of outside engineering and architectural firms who specialize in this type of review and are especially attuned to the needs of the lending community.

Cost Estimates

The review of the project's cost estimates should include an analysis of both direct (hard) costs and indirect (soft) costs of construction. The hard costs of construction include the actual costs for labor and materials as well as the general contractor's fee and any other charges directly relating to construction; for example, building permit fees, etc. Soft costs include such indirect construction costs as the amount paid by the developer for the land, interest charges on the loan, real estate taxes and assessments, attorneys' fees and any other costs and expenses necessary to complete the project which are not directly related to actual construction. The architect/engineer will generally limit his analysis to a review of the direct costs, whereas the review of the indirect costs is usually undertaken by more financially oriented personnel.

When the architect/engineer reviews the estimate of direct costs submitted by the borrower, his analysis forms should be geared to a line-by-line comparison with acknowledged trade cost estimates based upon the locality of the property and the type of construction called for by the plans and specifications. At this point, if the borrower's estimates approximate the architect/engineer's computation of costs, approval of the cost estimates will generally be granted. If there is a significant variance with either specific line items or the total projected costs, the borrower will be asked to submit evidence substantiating its cost figures. Such evidence may consist of executed construction contracts, if available, and/or bids from local subcontractors as well as progress schedules, construction techniques to be used (e.g., fast track construction) and quantities of materials to be ordered. This is necessary so that the architect/engineer will have sufficient information to determine whether the borrower is approaching the project in a reasonable manner. When reviewing these materials, the architect/engineer should give consideration to whether the borrower is also acting as its own general contractor, in which case, considerable cost savings can be achieved. Consideration must also be given to increasing the borrower's cost projections on individual subcontracts if they are lower than typical in the area.

The review of the progress schedules can be enlightening, especially when there is evidence that unusually large portions of the loan are to be drawn down in the early stages. An astute architect/engineer will readily detect front-loaded cost estimates which call for the subcontractors performing the initial work to be paid at significantly higher amounts than would normally be called for under the circumstances.

Plans and Specifications

The review by the architect/engineer of the plans and specifications will, as indicated, form the basis upon which to project estimated costs. It will also permit an analysis of the design of the project and a determination as to whether it will be structurally sound (assuming it is constructed in accordance with the plans and specifications). Since the construction lender is generally concerned with having the building completed in shell form, the focus of the architect/engineer's review will be concerned primarily with overall adequacy of design and compliance with governmental requirements. Detailed data concerning tenant finish work will usually not be an important factor at this stage unless it is an integral part of the acceptance of the overall plans and specifications by the provider of permanent financing. Thus, the focal points of the architect/engineer's review will be centered around the analysis of soil composition, structural and mechanical plans, site work and compliance with applicable building codes. Verification that the property and its intended use comply with applicable zoning regulations, including setback requirements and minimum parking requirements, and OSHA standards in the case of buildings designed for industrial use, etc., and compliance with environmental rules and regulations may also be included within the scope of the architect/engineer's review.

Basically, the overall scope and emphasis of the architect/engineer's review will depend on the individual policies of the particular lender. Many lenders have prescribed minimum standards for construction which, if not met, may preclude the issuance of a commitment. However, failure to meet all of the lender's standards will not necessarily result in an outright rejection of the borrower's loan application. The commitment may still be issued subject to receipt and satisfactory review of outstanding items, with the actual closing either delayed or provision made to have these outstanding items resolved shortly after closing.

Of course, the plans and specifications and any changes, must also be acceptable to and approved by the provider of take-out funds before the construction loan closes.

THE ROLE OF THE LENDER'S ATTORNEY IN THE LOAN UNDERWRITING PROCESS

For a construction lending program to work, competent legal support must be available to the construction lender. This may be in the form of in-house counsel or outside private law firms who have an expertise in the real estate area. In either case, the lender's counsel should be involved in the transaction at the earliest possible time in order to become familiar with the business aspects of the transaction and assist in structuring the loan.

Doing Business Requirements

One of the first issues that the lender's counsel must determine is whether the lender has authority to make and enforce the proposed loan. Several states impose restrictions on certain types of financing and have "doing business" requirements that affect construction lenders. For example, unless the lender is "qualified" to do business in the particular state, statutory provisions may prohibit the lender from enforcing its loan documents until it is so qualified. In certain cases, the time and expense involved in qualifying to do business may not justify the profit to be derived from the loan. Hence, the lawyer's advice is critical here before the lender gets too involved and is forced to qualify no matter what the cost.

Usury

The usury statutes of the state where the property is located must also be checked at the outset of the transaction. Certain states may impose usury ceilings that are unacceptable to construction lenders with today's fluctuating interest rates and variable interest loans. In addition, certain usury limitations may apply only to individuals as opposed to partnerships or corporations and an attorney's assistance at this stage could help in restructuring the composition of the borrower to comply with local laws. Similarly, when a recomposition of the borrowing entity will not suffice, the attorney could be invaluable in restructuring the entire transaction so that it becomes a so-called "out-of-state" transaction, not subject to the situs state's restrictive usury provisions.

Governmental Approvals

The attorney should also check out during the application process, the various permits and governmental approvals submitted with the applicant's papers. This will involve review of the building permit (or at least verification that it will be routinely issued after certain specified requirements are complied with) as well as the procedure for issuing the permit and verification that all appropriate agencies have approved the permit. It will also involve verification that all environmental and energy requirements necessary to complete the improvements have been obtained; although there never really can be any conclusive, definitive opinions given in this area, since lawsuits can always be filed contesting the validity of any requisite environmental impact report or alleging improper issuance of the permit, etc. The best advice the lender's attorney can give his client in this area is never to finance a project that would not be of benefit to the city in which it is being constructed.

Take-Out Commitment

Another important and critical function for the lender's counsel to perform during the loan underwriting process is to review the take-out commitment. The attorney must analyze the take-out commitment from a legal viewpoint to assure the lender that it is not filled with so many loopholes that it is "unbankable"; that is, unreliable as a form of take-out financing. The attorney should also alert the lender as to those requirements of the take-out commitment which should be addressed and if possible, satisfied at the early stages of the construction loan.

Other Matters

If there are leases affecting the property or other matters material to the transaction, for example, restrictive covenants, these must also be reviewed by the lender's counsel at the underwriting stage. Quite a few lenders have been very embarrassed when they go through all the complexities of making a loan and find, just before closing, that the leases or other matters are unacceptable to it and can't be changed, especially when the leases or the documentation reflecting the other matters have been sitting in the lender's files from the time the loan application was submitted.

Since lenders sometimes and often erroneously take the position that all matters affecting the transaction can be transformed to comply with their requirements, it becomes the main responsibility of the developer to highlight to the lender those items which will not be subject to amendment and must be accepted "as is" by the lender if it desires to make the construction loan. For example, if the property is preleased to a major creditworthy tenant, it may not be possible for the developer to effect changes to the lease to suit the requirements of the construction lender or the provider of take-out financing. Thus, the construction lender should review the leases before it gets too involved in the transaction and determine if they are acceptable to it and the take-out lender or purchaser. To do otherwise would place it in a position either of having to declare a default under its commitment for failure to satisfy the "acceptable leases" provision or of funding on a loan where all the ingredients are not acceptable to it.

The best way for the developer to resolve this possible future point of controversy and highlight the need for the lender to have its counsel review matters at an early stage, would be to condition the application (and subsequently, the developer's acceptance of the lender's commitment) on the acceptability of these items. Although lenders are not always willing to do this, a compromise is sometimes reached whereby the lender agrees in the commitment to return the developer's commitment fee in the event the specific items are not found acceptable within a certain period of time.

3
Structuring the Construction Loan

FACTORS TO BE CONSIDERED

After the basic loan underwriting has been completed, it becomes time to structure the construction loan so that the needs of both the borrower and the lender will be met. Consequently, final structuring of the construction loan will depend among other factors upon the nature of the proposed project; the borrowing entity and usury problems; the borrower's interest in the land; the amount and type of costs to be financed; the method of advancing funds; equity requirements for the borrower; whether or not there is permanent financing; the terms of the general contract; factors relating to the major subcontractors; requisite governmental approvals; the security for the loan, special events of default and potential title problems. The variables are infinite, and as with most other things, will depend ultimately upon the exact nature of the transaction and the general lending policy of the lender as well as the relative bargaining power of the borrower and lender.

Nature of Proposed Project

The nature of the proposed project, as stated, will be a factor to be considered in structuring the construction loan. Different considerations govern the making of a residential loan or an office building loan, or whether a shopping center, factory, warehouse, hotel or other type of commercial project is contemplated. For example, if an inner city office building is planned, the lender may condition its approval

STRUCTURING THE CONSTRUCTION LOAN 37

upon a parking garage being built (by third persons or the city). If a warehouse is contemplated, the lender may insist upon a railroad connection via a spur track, and so on. In many instances, if the project is to be sold ultimately in condominium units, the lender may require a certain number of units to be pre-sold before advancing a particular level of funds or releasing any retainage. Similarly, preleasing in office buildings may play the same role.

Borrowing Entity and Usury Problems

The nature of the borrowing entity may give rise to possible usury problems in several states. This could be the cause of structuring the loan as an out-of-state transaction, if possible, or alternately, requiring that the loan be entered into by an entity barred from asserting usury as a defense. The role of the attorney in the underwriting process will be critical in determining whether any structuring along these lines will be necessary, and if so that it be done lawfully.

Borrower's Interest

The borrower's interest in the property, be it a fee interest, leasehold interest or a combination of both, will of necessity be a factor in structuring the loan. When the borrower has fee simple title to the land the approach of the lender is fairly straightforward. However, if the fee interest is subject to the air rights of a third party or other title restrictions, the type and size of construction may be affected. Similarly, if the borrower has a leasehold interest, the nature of the construction may be restricted by the ground lease. In addition, the lender must determine whether it is willing to make the construction loan on the basis of an unsubordinated or subordinated fee interest. In these situations the requirements and controls for construction should be consistent with possible title limitations and lease restrictions so as not to create a default under the terms of the governing documents.

Costs to be Financed

The lender must determine at the outset whether it intends to finance land acquisition costs and/or whether soft costs will be financed along with the hard construction costs. In relation to the cost estimates, this will establish the amount of equity funds or secondary gap financing needed by the developer. The lender must then structure its loan to provide for infusion of these funds into the project, either at the inception of the loan, before the lender's funds are used or in stages during construction. Sometimes lenders will accept letters of credit to cover the differences between the estimated costs and the construction loan proceeds, which will be drawn upon as and when needed after exhausting the lender's funds. Depending upon the particular lending institution involved, certain lenders may be restricted from funding on specified, nonqualified costs of construction (typically in the soft cost area) which will play a factor in the lender's determination of what costs it will fund. The existence and terms of any permanent financing will also be an essential consideration in this regard.

Method of Advancing Funds

The lender's prescribed method of advancing funds will also be a factor to be considered in structuring the construction loan. Funds are typically advanced against paid receipts and vouchers and/or as a percentage of completion. It is customary for 10% of hard construction costs to be retained, with the lender funding 100% of the soft costs included in the lender's construction budget. These percentages may vary, and depending in part upon the nature of the transaction (and, of course, there being no default under the loan), lenders may agree to disburse 50% (or some other percentage) of the retainage upon 50% completion or release the retainage altogether as to specific trades when everyone in the particular trade has completed its work for the project. It is usually preferable for the lender's requirements for advancing funds to be consistent with the terms of the general contract and any statutory requirements providing for holdbacks to create a fund for suppliers of labor or material who are not in privity with the owner.

Equity Requirements For the Borrower

The amount of money, if any, to be put into the project by the borrower, as well as the time and for what purposes the equity money is to be applied, is dependent upon the total estimated costs for the project and the lender's determination of what costs and how much of the project it desires to finance. The desires and financial capability of the borrower will, of course, also be material aspects in this determination, with all of the various ingredients balanced to come up with an appropriate equity contribution. Oftentimes, the borrower's equity money is used to fund certain nonqualified costs that the lender is prohibited from funding against.

Permanent Financing

The existence of permanent financing is a material consideration during the loan underwriting stage and is also a material factor in structuring the loan. The amount of the permanent financing will most probably set the total amount of the construction loan (unless gap financing is available) and the funding requirements, for example, the criteria for floor funding and for funding in stages, should restrict the total amount of construction loan proceeds that the construction lender will permit to be outstanding at any particular time. Any special requirements of the permanent financing will also have to be considered by the construction lender and should be incorporated into the terms of the construction loan. The construction loan should also be structured so that the approval of the provider of permanent financing will be required for all matters susceptible of approval by it at the outset of the construction loan and for any subsequent changes in the construction loan that may affect the permanent financing commitment.

General Contract

The provisions of the general contract regarding payment terms (e.g., fixed price, scheduled payments, cost plus or other) will have a bearing on the lender's method of advancing funds as well as the possible equity requirements for the borrower. Similarly, the retainage provisions concerning percentage retained and when payable should be consistent (as should the payment terms) with the lender's requirements so that the borrower is not squeezed between its obligations to effect payment under the construction contract and its right to receive funds from the lender.

Major Subcontracts

The provisions of the major subcontracts, like those of the general contract, may also be a factor in structuring the construction loan. The principal terms to focus upon in major subcontracts are those relating to form and method of payment, retainage and work covered. These should be consistent with the general contract, and in turn, be consistent with the lender's method of advancing funds.

Government Approvals

It goes without saying that the construction loan must be structured to be in compliance with governmental rules and regulations. These may relate to zoning and environmental restrictions, applicable Urban Development Action Grant (UDAG), Urban Development Corporation (UDC) or Federal Housing Administration (FHA) requirements, and/or tax abatement provisions, and so on. Basically, within reasonable limits, the construction lender should work with the developer to insure that the various rules and regulations are complied with and maximum advantage is derived from any benefits to be had.

Security for the Loan

The security for the construction loan will almost certainly consist of a mortgage on the borrower's interest in the land and, depending upon various circumstances, may also consist of payment and performance bonds, guarantees of payment and completion (or other matters), letters of credit, pledge of stock or other personalty including the assignment of interests in a corporate borrower or guarantor and possibly negative pledge agreements. The requisite security must be factored into the loan structuring and as will most factors, be an outcrop of the various aspects of loan underwriting. In addition, to avoid potential conflicts, lenders may structure the loan so that any funding for non-qualified costs is secured by non real estate collateral.

Special Events of Default

When the lender has other deals with the borrower, or the development is an integral part of an existing or to be developed project, among other factors, the lender may call for certain specified extraneous events to be considered defaults under its loan. This is typified by cross-defaults with other loans or may be reflected in separate agreements tied by reference into the construction loan documents.

Potential Title Problems

Applicable mechanic's lien statutes will result in the loan being structured so that potential problems are either minimized or eliminated. For example, in New York, construction loan proceeds are customarily disbursed in trust in order to maintain the priority of the mortgage pursuant to the state's applicable mechanics lien provisions. In other states, the lender may want to disburse funds through the title company rather than directly to the borrower, in order to insure that continued title insurance coverage against mechanics lien claims is maintained.

Other title problems, for example, easements or restrictive covenants, and so on, can usually be guarded against by insuring that the contemplated structure and its use conform to any applicable restrictions and obtaining affirmative title insurance if available.

Other Factors

Since no two projects are exactly the same, it is impossible to list all the factors that must be taken into account in structuring a construction loan. The foregoing represented merely those factors most commonly considered by construction lenders, and even they may not be applicable to all transactions. The ultimate factors that will play a role in the loan structuring will depend, as with most other matters, on the specifics of the deal and the nature and policies of the parties involved.

SELECTED PROBLEMS

Many areas of construction lending deserve special attention in order to minimize the risk to the construction lender. There are several problem areas of exceeding importance such as those that relate to: (1) nonqualified costs; (2) priority of the lender's lien as respects subsequent or existing mechanics liens; (3) contracts to which the lender is not a party; (4) matters over which the borrower has no written contractual control; (5) the permanent take-out commitment; (6) the time when the project is almost completed and (7) leasehold loans.

Nonqualified Costs

There are certain costs related to the construction loan which, depending upon the state involved and the particular type of lender, may not be considered "qualified"; that is, costs permitted to be funded by the lender. (REITs in particular are concerned with the possibility of making prohibited personal property loans.) These costs usually relate to soft costs as opposed to the hard costs of construction and typically involve funding for land acquisition, attorneys fees and so on. The consequence to lenders for funding on these so-called nonqualified costs may be an outright prohibition against enforcing any security interests and/or the placement of the loan into a limited "basket" type category. It may also taint the loan as far as priority versus mechanics liens is concerned.

The lender should require that the borrower's equity be used to fund nonqualified costs to avoid the problem. If this is not possible, funding for the nonqualified costs should be secured with non-real-estate collateral as a separate loan, with separate loan agreements (including separate mortgages) entered into. To prevent funding for nonqualified items as construction progresses, a schedule of the soft cost items to be funded should be attached as a schedule to the building loan agreement.

Priority Versus Mechanics' Liens

The priority of the liens of laborers and materialmen in relation to the construction lender's lien and security interest, is established by state constitutions and statutes. Consequently, the necessary protective steps to be taken by the lender will differ from state to state. A more detailed analysis of this area can be found in chapter 7. Suffice it to say

Contracts To Which The Lender Is Not A Party

Every construction project will involve contracts between the borrower and architects, engineers, contractors and tenants, etc., to which the lender is not a party. The problem the lender faces is in enforcing these contracts in the event the borrower defaults under them and/or under the construction loan. This takes on particular significance when the lender has to take over completion of the project and costs for labor and materials have increased considerably from the time the original contracts were entered into.

To enhance the lender's position, it should require as a condition of its commitment that such parties provide the lender with written notice and an opportunity to cure any defaults beyond the period permitted the borrower to cure defaults under the respective contracts. This condition should be supplemented with the requirement that in the event of any foreclosure, the contracting parties will undertake to complete their contracts at no additional charge provided the lender, the lender's nominee or a purchaser at foreclosure sale complies with its portion of the contract. The contractors should also be prohibited from looking to the lender for any payments due them from the borrower for work that the lender had previously advanced funds for out of the construction loan.

Matters Over Which the Borrower Has No Written Contractual Control

Occasionally, items important to the project will arise over which the borrower has no written contractual control. For example, in the case of a large regional shopping center, a major tenant may require that it build its own building, even though the building will be owned by the borrower and only leased to the tenant. In this situation, neither the borrower nor the lender would be in privity with the tenant's contractor. A subsequent default by the tenant could preclude completion of the tenant's building, which if required by the take-out commitment, would place the entire project in jeopardy. The solution here is very similar to that called for in the preceding paragraph, but adding the lender as a third-party beneficiary to the tenant's contract.

Permanent Take-Out Commitment

The importance of the permanent take-out commitment to the construction lender cannot be overemphasized. Consequently, the construction lender must do everything possible prior to opening its loan, to insure that any ambiguities between the borrower and provider of take-out funds are resolved and that all the requirements of the take-out commitment that can be complied with at such time are in fact satisfied. However, there will always be conditions of the take-out commitment that cannot be met until completion of construction.

One such condition, customarily found in all take-out commitments, is that construction be completed in accordance with the plans and specifications approved by the provider of take-out funds. Although initial approval of the plans and specifications can and should be obtained, there are always "change orders" in any construction project, which if material, could serve to void the permanent take-out commitment unless the approval of the provider of take-out funds is obtained in each instance.

To avoid the time consuming and administratively burdensome task of obtaining the provider of take-out funds approval for each change order and to minimize disputes over what change orders are "material," the construction lender should require that the borrower and provider of take-out funds agree on a flexible formula for approving changes in plans and specifications. For example, the provider of take-out funds could agree in advance to any change orders that do not diminish the number of square feet in the building and/or the amount of the construction costs below certain limits. Specifically approved change orders submitted prior to the foregoing limits being exceeded would then serve to automatically renew the preapproval arrangement within the permissible limits.

In order to establish that the construction lender acted in reliance upon the take-out commitment, the construction lender should obtain an assignment of the commitment from the borrower, with the provider of take-out funds acknowledging the assignment and entering into a triparty agreement with the borrower and construction lender. (See chapter 8 for a more detailed discussion of this subject.)

The Time When The Project Is Almost Completed

The time when the project is almost but not quite finished may be particularly troublesome. The work remaining is usually detailed and although not particularly time consuming, needs to be done at a time when the contractors are anxious to remove their crews and go on to other projects. To insure that the final stages of construction get the proper attention, the construction lender's best weapon is the retainage provisions in the construction loan documents and the construction contracts themselves. Preferably, the retainage provisions should call for the withholding of funds until all tenants have approved their spaces *and* until the provider of take-out funds has accepted construction as being completed in accordance with the accepted plans and specifications. Additional preconditions for the release of the retainage could call for the tenants actually to be paying rent under their leases and/or for all the remaining requirements of the permanent take-out commitment to be fulfilled. However, it should be noted that exceptions to these somewhat stringent requirements can and do take place.

Leasehold Loans

Construction loans secured by leasehold as opposed to fee interests in realty present special problems which must be addressed at the outset if the construction lender does not want to risk losing its security. The problem stems from the fact that the lender's security is based upon the borrower's leasehold interest in the property. Should the borrower default under its lease and the lease be terminated, the borrower no longer has an interest in the property and the lender's security disappears. This puts a premium on resolving all ambiguities in the lease and, if possible, amending unfavorable lease provisions.

In this type of situation, the construction lender should require as a bare minimum that the lessor/owner of the property agree that any attempted termination of the lease and/or any notice of default served on the lessee/borrower shall not be valid unless the lessor first provides the lender with notice and a reasonable time in which to cure any such defaults. In addition, the lessor/owner should agree that in the event the lender institutes foreclosure proceedings against the lessee/borrower's leasehold interest, the lender or its nominee, or the purchaser at a foreclosure sale can become a substitute tenant. If the lessor/owner refuses to agree to these provisions, the construction lender should *not* close its loan.*

For this reason, among others, borrowers who are entering into leases which they intend later to serve as collateral for construction loans, should consider the probable requirements of a potential construction lender prior to finalizing the lease terms.

---

*The best approach to leasehold situations would be to require a rider to the ground lease providing that during the pendency of lenders' interests (both construction and long-term), the lease may not be terminated or occupancy thereunder interrupted except for nonpayment of rent, taxes and insurance and in any such case, only 30 days after notice has been *received* by lender; and that the lessee's interests thereunder are freely assignable and mortgageable; and, that the premises may be used for any lawful pupose. Otherwise the lessor's position should be subordinated to the lender's position.

4
Loan Participations

WHY PARTICIPATE?

The typical form of construction loan participation customarily provides for one lender, the "lead lender," to sell an interest or interests in a construction loan together with the security given therefore, to one or more other lenders, the "participants," with the lead lender continuing to service the loan for the benefit of all lenders involved.

There are a variety of reasons why a lead lender would sell one or more participations in a loan rather than retaining a 100% interest and they depend upon the particular circumstances of the transaction and of the lender. Some of the advantages to the lead lender in selling participations include the ability of the lead lender to (1) diversify its loan portfolio; (2) make loans in excess of its legal and/or internal lending limitations; (3) obtain a greater return on its funds resulting from interest overrides or disproportionately greater commitment fees earned as finder or as servicer of the loan; (4) increase the effective rate of return by controlling the timing of advances and (5) maintain client relationships despite a shortage of funds.

On the other hand, participants also derive benefits from entering into loan participations, some of which include the ability to: (1) diversify their loan portfolios; (2) overcome usury problems in states which favor domestic lenders; (3) avoid the necessity of servicing loans and (4) make indirect investments in jurisdictions where direct investment would be prohibited.

Advantages to the Lead Lender

Diversification of Loan Portfolio. Lenders are generally restricted in the type and size of the transactions they may finance. This is partly by choice, but also as a result of the limited amount of capital that they may have available for construction lending. By selling off portions of loans, lead lenders overcome the limited availability of capital and become able to enter into both more and larger type deals. By spreading the "risk," they are also able to enter into specialty areas of construction, for example, hospital or hotel construction in which they would not get involved otherwise.

Lending Limitations. Many states (and the federal government) limit the amount of funds that a lender under its jurisdiction may invest in any one particular transaction to a percentage of the lender's capital. These limitations also may be tied to a percentage of the appraised value of the property itself or to the percentage of the lender's assets that may be invested in that class of security. In any case, this legal lending limitation would hamper the construction of many of today's $100 million plus deals if not for the use of this method of participating plus the availability of loan participants.

Similarly, many institutions have their own internal guidelines limiting their dollar exposure per transaction. These limitations may be expressed as a cap on the percentage of assets that may go into any one project or to any one borrower, or may be stated in terms of an absolute dollar limitation, depending on the institution. In any event, the result is the same. By entering into loan participations, these lenders are able to cause loans to be made that would otherwise be in excess of their lending limitations.

Greater Returns on Investment. In most situations, the lead lender will be the "finder" of the loan and will be servicing the loan. To compensate it for these functions, the lead lender often receives an interest override; that is, interest in excess of that payable to the participants and/or a disproportionately greater share of the commitment fee paid by the borrower. This results in a better return to the lead lender than it otherwise would have received had it not participated in the loan with others.

Increase Effective Rate of Return. In addition to receiving a greater return on its investment, the lead lender is also able to increase its overall effective rate of return by controlling the timing of advances. Generally, the lead lender will advance funds to the borrower and then request proportionate reimbursement from the participants. This enables the lead lender to have its funds out "first" and earning a return at the earliest possible time. The lead lender, within reason, will also be able to determine the actual disbursement dates and thus better coordinate its construction advances with its inflow of funds.

Client Relationships. When a lender is short of capital and a developer applies for a construction loan, the lender will be faced with a difficult decision. If it declines the developer's application, the developer will almost surely go to a competing lender and the first lender risks either the loss of a valued customer and/or the failure to gain a new one. On the other hand, should the lender accept and fund the entire application, it risks using up scarce resources and/or overextending itself. This in turn may place the lender in a position of not being able to fulfill its other commitments, an intolerable position for a lender. The logical answer supplied by many is to accept the application and sell off participations in the loan. This way capital necessary for other projects is preserved and good client relationships are maintained.

Advantages to the Participants

Diversification of Loan Portfolio. Participants have the same concerns regarding diversity of loan portfolio as do lead lenders. In particular, by purchasing a portion of the loan, the participant can partake in certain transactions in reliance upon the expertise of the lead lender. This allows the participant to share in the construction financing of different types of projects, thus lessening the impact on it from any downturns in specific areas of real estate financing; for example, office versus apartment financing.

Usury Problems. There are certain states that favor domestic lenders in their usury laws. California was a perfect example of this until recent changes in the state usury provisions. Certain exempted categories of lenders were permitted to make loans at almost any interest rate while most foreign lenders were subject to severe usury limitations. Thus, for such lenders to make high interest loans in California, it was necessary that they not be the originator of the loan. In most cases a California bank would make the loan, thereby purging the loan of the taint of usury, and sell off participations to lenders outside the state. This practice was fairly widespread in California, although there was never a true consensus among the legal community as to its propriety in the eyes of the California courts. Fortunately for lenders, the matter was never judicially resolved against them.

Servicing Loans. Many lenders have no facilities to service loans. They either do not have the manpower, equipment or expertise to handle the essential functions satisfactorily, or they are unfamiliar with the specific type of property involved. Since most lead lenders also service the loans, the participation arrangement is an excellent vehicle to resolve this problem for the participants. In fact, the lead lender has substantial interest in serving each loan properly as an owner of a portion of the investment with its own money at risk.

Indirect Investments. Certain states differentiate between classes of lenders and the types of investments in which these classes may partake directly. However, if the loan is made by a qualified lender, there is usually no prohibition against the unqualified lender indirectly sharing in the investment. This may be simply accomplished through the participation vehicle, with results very similar to overcoming certain states' usury limitations, as previously mentioned.

COMMITMENT

Generally, the commitment to make the construction loan is issued by the lead lender; although, on occasion, the commitment is issued jointly by the lead lender and the participant. It is not uncommon for the lead lender to condition its commitment upon the approval and acceptance of all commitment conditions by the participant, particularly when the lead lender would be unwilling to make the loan without other parties participating in the funding.

PARTICIPATION CERTIFICATE

The loan documents are usually recorded in the name of the lead lender, with the participants' interests in the loan evidenced by participation certificates issued by the lead lender at the time of each advance.

THE PARTICIPATION AGREEMENT

The relationship between the lead lender and the participant will be governed by the terms of a participation agreement usually entered into prior to or simultaneously with the closing of the loan. If the lead lender ultimately intends to sell participations, clearance of all the loan documents with the known participants and agreement upon the forms of such documents and the participation agreement before closing may save a lot of embarrassment and problems should there be disputes between the lead lender and the participants after loan closing.

A participation agreement will typically contain among others, provisions relating to (1) the percentage interest in the loan owned by each party; (2) disbursement of the loan proceeds; (3) representations and warranties of the lead lender or the participant; (4) servicing of the loan by the lead lender; (5) prohibition against assignment of either party's interest in the loan to a third party; (6) disposition of the loan in the event of default by the participating parties.

Percentage Interest in the Loan

The participation agreement will set forth each party's percentage interest in the loan and will usually provide for the lead lender and participant to fund their percentage interests proportionately at the time of each construction loan advance; or alternately, for the participant to reimburse the lead lender for its proportionate share of advances made to date and promise to fund its share in the future within a specified time after receipt of notice that an advance had been made.

The lead lender and participant will generally share in the payments made under the loan agreements in accordance with their respective percentage interests, subject to any interest override and/or disproportionately greater amount of any commitment fee received from the borrower that may be due the lead lender.

Disbursement of Loan Proceeds

Provisions relating to disbursement of the loan proceeds vary and will depend, to a large extent, on the relationship between the lead lender and participant. Generally, the lead lender either disburses the complete draw request to the borrower and receives prompt reimbursement from the participant equal to its percentage interest in the loan, or each party disburses on notice its proportionate share only directly to the borrower or an escrow agent such as the title company.

Problems and delays in funding are often encountered when participants insist on duplicating the approval process for the borrower's draw requests already performed by the lead lender. The latter review process becomes particularly burdensome if more than one participant is involved, although the delays can possibly be shortened by having the borrower submit copies of the supporting data simultaneously to all interested parties. However, lead lenders and borrowers, too, sometimes regard their relationships as personal and may object to any other contacts.

The most efficient way for draw requests to be processed would seem to be by submitting them directly to the lead lender. The lead lender would then review the data and after approving disbursement, notify the participant of the funds required and perhaps (but not in every case) furnish the participant with copies of the submitted material. The participant would then arrange to wire transfer its proportionate share of the disbursement to the lead lender's account within the agreed-to period following receipt of notice that the lead lender is making a disbursement to the borrower. The supporting material, if not already reviewed, would be reviewed thereafter by the participant prior to the next draw request; and, if there are any problems, they can be resolved in sufficent time so as not to delay the next funding. In this manner, there are no unnecessary delays to funding although the participant is, at least to the extent of one draw request, relying upon the good judgment of the lead lender. Exceptions can always be made where justified by a recent past history of problems or where the particular draw is a substantial part of the total amount of the loan.

Representations and Warranties

Participants who are looking to the expertise of the lead lender will seek representations and warranties as to: the value of the property; the solvency of the borrower; the legality of the loan documents; the loan not being in default (in the case of existing loans); the authority of the lead lender to enter into the transaction; the current status of the improvements and the sufficiency of the funds available to complete the project. On the other hand, lead lenders are almost universally insistent that they are not insurers of the loan; and, therefore, the participants must make their own investigations as to the foregoing matters. Thus, it is not uncommon to see the representations and warranties of the lead lender limited to the fact that they have the requisite loan documents and will maintain same in their possession throughout the loan and that to the best of their knowledge the borrower is not insolvent, that they have the requisite authority to make the loan, and where the loan is already in existence, that they have not declared any defaults thereunder (if such is the case) and to the best of their knowledge, there exists no current defaults. Any other course may lead to involving the lead lender in a "security" problem coming under the Federal Security Acts, especially where there is a disparity in the sophistication of the lead lender and the participant.

Servicing

Since lead lenders usually obtain an interest override or higher proportion of the commitment fee, they generally agree to service the loan without further charge. Servicing includes collecting payments due under the loan and remitting to the participants their percentage interests in such payments. The servicing function will also include the responsibility to discharge the obligations of the mortgagee or trust deed beneficiary named in the loan documents. However, astute lead lenders will set a standard for their servicing function by providing that they are responsible for no higher degree of care in servicing the loan than that provided for in the servicing of their other investments.

Assignment

Most participation agreements contain some form of prohibition against the assignment of any party's interest in the loan without the other party's approval. This provision is especially important to the participant who might not have purchased a portion of the loan if it were not for the expertise of the lead lender. Alternately, the lead lender wants a participant with whom it has, or can establish a good working relationship with so that the loan can be administered smoothly. The lead lender must also be sure that any participant will have the financial ability to make the required advances under the loan. However, a participant may at some point desire (or, in fact need) to raise capital by selling its interest in the loan and does not want to be dependent upon the lead lender for the ability to do this. To reconcile these conflicting interests, the right to approve assignments is often qualified with the words "such approval not to be unreasonably withheld." Sometimes net worth requirements for a prospective participation purchaser are also established. A frequent provision found in participation agreements concerning a sale of the lead lender's interest will permit such sale provided the lead lender retains its capacity as lead and keeps a certain minimum percentage of the loan. This provision is usually found in situations where the lead lender knows at the outset of the transaction that it intends to sell additional participations at a later date.

Default By the Borrower

The provisions in the participation agreement relating to default by the borrower deal with the requirement of notice to participants and the enforcement of remedies in the event of such default. Generally, lead lenders will obligate themselves promptly to notify each participant of any default or other matter which may *materially* affect the loan or the interest of the participant in the loan. They will also agree to the extent possible, to notify the participant prior to exercising any remedies under the loan documents or making payments to third persons to protect the security (e.g., such as taxes, insurance premiums, prior mortgage charges or rent). The lead lender would be seeking reimbursement from the participant for its proportionate share of advances to third parties and should be careful to give adequate notice so as not to get into a dispute over the propriety of any such advances.

The latitude given the lead lender in enforcing the default provisions of the loan documents will vary from agreement to agreement and will, to a great extent, depend upon the percentage interest in the loan held by each party. Although the lead lender will most likely want complete discretion in handling default situations (based upon a standard relating to the lead lender's handling of its own loans) this will rarely be granted in situations where the participant (or participants collectively) has a majority interest in the loan. On the other hand, where the lead lender has retained the major portion of the loan, it will almost certainly insist upon the broadest possible authority to work out default situations. Nonetheless, a compromise should be reached where the parties will agree that in the event of default by the borrower they will pursue a course of action acceptable to all parties; and, if such agreement cannot be reached, the loan documents will be enforced as written unless countermanded by the owners of two-thirds or some larger fraction of the loan. This is why participants and lead lenders would be wise to pick partners whom they trust and with whom they can work in both good times and bad. This is also one of the most critical areas of the participation agreement, for the lead lender might have other ongoing interests with the borrower (especially if the lead lender is a bank), and may be reluctant to pursue foreclosure proceedings aggressively if they would cause the borrower to "go under" and thus jeopardize such other interests. There may be a real conflict here between the interests of the lead lender and the participant which should be addressed and resolved, if possible, in the participation agreement.

Default By Either Party to the Participation Agreement

Under most circumstances, the only default that can be made by a participant would be its inability or willful refusal to fulfill its commitment to advance funds as construction progresses. The lead lender, on the other hand, can be in default under the agreement for breach of warranty or representation, failure to properly service the loan or enforce the loan documents as provided or otherwise fail to perform acts called for under the agreement.

To cover these default situations, the agreement may contain various damage provisions permitting either party to seek its remedies at law or possibly through arbitration. More probably, the damage provisions will require the defaulting party to purchase the interest of the aggrieved party at par plus accrued interest, and/or permit the aggrieved party to purchase the interest of the defaulting party at par plus accrued interest if the defaulting party is unable to respond. It is not common for the participation agreement to permit either party to seek damages for loss of bargain or specific performance.

Other Provisions

Customarily, the participation agreement will contain additional "boiler plate" provisions dealing with the governing law, wiring instructions for credits and payments to be made under the loan and ruling out oral modification as well as other matters that will for the most part depend upon the particulars of the transaction.

Form of Agreement

A form of participation agreement used by a lender that customarily purchases 90% of a loan as a participant, together with a rider to be attached to the agreement and a participation certificate are appended at the end of this chapter for reference use. These documents were designed for a strong, major (and sole) participant with significant control over the transaction and should be read bearing these facts in mind. In addition, as with any form, it should be used only as a guide to be adapted to the specific circumstances pertaining to the loan and the relationship between the parties.

PARTICIPATION AGREEMENT

THIS AGREEMENT made and entered into this   day of

19   , by and between

(hereinafter referred to as "Lender") and

having its principal place of business at
            (hereinafter referred to as "Participant").

𝔚𝔦𝔱𝔫𝔢𝔰𝔰𝔢𝔱𝔥:

WHEREAS, Lender has made, or is a participant in, a first mortgage construction loan ("the Loan") in the principal amount of $, of which $ has heretofore been advanced to the borrower named on Schedule "A" hereto ("the Borrower"), which schedule also contains a description of the property which is security for the Loan ("the Property"), the document providing such security, the name of any guarantors of the Loan and other pertinent information relating to the Loan and the Property, all of which is incorporated herein with the same force and effect as though set forth in full herein; and

WHEREAS, Lender is the sole owner of the Loan or, if not the sole owner of the Loan, of an undivided interest therein of dignity and lien priority equal to that of the other owners thereof, and has not pledged or assigned in interest in the Loan; and

WHEREAS, Lender desires to sell and Participant desires to purchase, an undivided interest in the Loan on the terms and conditions hereinafter set forth:

NOW, THEREFORE, in consideration of the mutual covenants, agreements and provisions herein contained, the parties hereto do hereby covenant and agree as follows:

1. Subject to the terms and provisions of this agreement, the Lender hereby sells and Participant hereby purchases an undivided interest in the Loan equal to   % ("the Percentage") of the amount advanced and to be advanced on the Loan. Participant shall pay for such undivided interest the sum of $ representing the Percentage of the amount heretofore advanced on the Loan and shall also pay the Percentage of the amounts hereafter advanced but in no event shall participant be required to pay more than a total of $ for such undivided interest. Participant shall pay the initial portion of such purchase price by cash or check against the delivery to it by Lender of a participation certificate in form and substance mutually satisfactory to Lender and Participant evidencing the undivided interest of Participant in the Loan. Such certificate shall show the Percentage of the Loan owned by Participant and shall also indicate that such participation is subject to the terms and conditions of this agreement. The interest of Lender and Participant in the Loan shall be of equal lien and neither party shall have any priority over the other. Further payments by Participant for such undivided interest, based on advances hereafter made to the Borrower in accordance with the Loan documents, shall be made after notice from Lender given not less than forty-eight hours prior to the time such advances are to be made.

2. Lender represents, warrants and agrees that it presently has (or will have when Participant first acquires an interest in the Loan) and will have at the time of each advance to the Borrower, in its possession, the following original executed documents relating to the Loan (except where copies are hereinafter specified or where the originals have been duly filed with appropriate officials) and that such documents or copies (by which it is intended to mean true and complete copies) are and will be as specifically represented in each of the following subparagraphs of this paragraph 2; provided, however, that if Lender is itself a participant, Lender only represents, warrants and agrees that it has verified (or will have verified when Participant first acquires an interest in the Loan) and will verify at the time of each advance to the Borrower, that the holder of the Loan ("the Lead Bank" identified in Schedule "A") has such documents (as so represented) in its possession:

(a) a note, bond or other obligation and a mortgage, deed of trust or similar instrument securing such obligation, more particularly indentified in Schedule "A", which are valid and binding on the parties thereto and enforceable in accordance with their terms; also a building loan contract or the equivalent, any consent by stockholders required by law and any required certifications as to resolutions of the Board of Directors of corporate borrowers and guarantors, all in form and substance satisfactory to counsel to the Lender,

(b) a title policy, title report, title binder or other binding written evidence of title insurance issued by the title insurance company or companies named in Schedule "A" which insures that the Lender (or, if Lender is a participant, that the Lead Bank) is the holder of a first priority real estate mortgage on the Property free of all liens and encumbrances and free of all liens arising by reason of unpaid bills or claims for work performed or materials furnished in connection with the improvements being constructed, and if such evidence of title insurance contains exceptions for restrictive covenants or other rights of third parties which might adversely affect title, such evidence of insurance shall also include, with respect to the restrictive covenants, affirmative insurance that they have not been violated and that any violation will not result in a forfeiture or reversion of title, or, with respect to such other rights, affirmative insurance that they will not be so enforced and shall contain no limitation, exception or reservation (nor reflect or recite any such limitation, exception or reservation) other than (i) utility easements fairly located and insured as so located which do not interfere with the position or intended use of the improvements or those to be constructed; (ii) such restrictive covenants as so insured; and (iii) leases and any other exception, reservation or limitation which have had the specific written approval of the person or persons issuing the take-out commitment or commitment for long-term financing. Such title policy, report or binder has been and will be appropriately updated or endorsed as of the time of each advance;

(c) an insurance policy or policies issued by the company or companies identified in Schedule "A" insuring against loss or damage by fire and against such other risks as are included in a broad form extended coverage endorsement with vandalism and malicious mischief endorsements covering all of the buildings and structures on the property, including such insurance on the Builder's Risk-Completed Value form on the improvements being constructed on the Property described in the plans and specifications identified in Schedule "A" ("the Improvements") and insuring the Lender (or the Lead Bank) for not less than the principal amount of the Loan from time to time outstanding.

(d) a copy of a current survey of the Property showing no variations and no encroachments which would render title unmarketable, which survey has been and will be appropriately updated during the course of construction of the Improvements;

(e) copies of all leases or subleases with tenants who are to occupy a material portion of the Improvements or which are required as a condition of the Permanent Commitment referred to in subparagraph (1) hereof;

(f) copies of the plans and specifications referred to in Schedule "A", together with authorization from the architect who prepared the same authorizing their use by the Lender (or the Lead Bank) in the event of default;

(g) a construction contract in customary form requiring the Improvements to be completed prior to expiration of the said Permanent Commitment and prior to the commencement date of the leases referred to in subparagraph (e) hereof, subject to delays deemed usually acceptable in the construction industry; and an assignment of such contract to the Lender (or the Lead Bank) effective in the event of a default in the Loan;

(h) a completion or performance and payment bond(s), as may be indicated in Schedule "A", from the surety company named in Schedule "A", such bond(s) naming the Lender (or the Lead Bank) as an obligee and, in the case of a completion bond, being written in such form that if the Borrower defaults under the terms of the mortgage or any building loan contract the surety company will accept full responsibility for completion or, in the case of performance and payment bonds, being written on A.I.A. Form A311, F.H.A. Form No. 2452 or an equivalent form;

(i) an appraisal of the Property with the Improvements, on a when-completed basis, rendered by a reputable MAI appraiser or a person of equal stature or experience, identified in Schedule "A", which appraisal shall be in an amount not less than 133% of the principal amount of the Loan;

(j) a copy of a building permit and evidence that the Improvements will comply with all applicable zoning laws;

(k) a certificate of an architect approved by Lender (or by the Lead Bank) showing that the amount advanced on the Loan represents not more than the value of the Improvements in place or delivered to and left upon the Property and that the undisbursed portion of the Loan is sufficient to complete the Improvements in timely manner in accordance with the plans and specifications identified on Schedule "A" which certificate shall be updated at the time of each advance;

(l) the unexpired valid commitment from the institution identified on Schedule "A" for a takeout mortgage loan ("the Permanent Commitment") in a minimum or floor amount of not less than the principal amount of the Loan, payable on completion of construction; and a buy-sell agreement with the issuer of the Permanent Commitment;

(m) if the Property or any portion thereof comprises a leasehold estate, a copy of the lease and of each modification or amendment thereof and of any mortgage, deed of trust or other encumbrance on the fee underlying such leasehold, which contain provisions adequate and sufficient, in the opinion of counsel to the Lender, to enable the Lender (or the Lead Bank) to take action within a reasonable time after the occurrence of a default in any of the provisions of the instrument in question to cure such default before it can result in termination, forfeiture or foreclosure of such leasehold estate and, if there are any events of default which are impossible of cure by Lender (or the Lead Bank) there are other provisions, adequate and sufficient in the opinion of said counsel, which enable Lender (or the Lead Bank) to preserve such leasehold estate, or to acquire a new equivalent leasehold estate in lieu thereof, notwithstanding such an event of default.

3. Lender agrees to hold the documents referred to in paragraph 2 hereof (or represents that the Lead Bank has agreed with Lender that it shall hold such documents, as set forth in a participation agreement, a copy of which is attached hereto) and agrees (or represents) that none of such documents shall (or may) be pledged, assigned, transferred or modified without the prior written consent of the Participant nor shall Lender (or the Lead Bank) make or consent to any release of the Borrower from any liability thereunder or waive any claim against the Borrower or any obligor under said documents or against any guarantor of the liabilities thereunder. Lender agrees to furnish to Participant promptly after request true and correct copies of all documents executed and delivered in connection with the Loan, including, without limitation, the documents described in paragraph 2 hereof and the plans and specifications described in Schedule "A".

4. The Loan shall be serviced by Lender (or, if Lender itself is a participant, by the Lead Bank) continuously from the date hereof without charge to Participant. Lender will proceed diligently to collect all payments due under the loan (or its participation therein) as and when the same shall become due and payable and will promptly discharge all of the obligations of mortgagee or beneficiary named in the instrument given as security for the Loan (except where Lender is itself a participant in which event it will cause the Lead Bank to discharge such obligations). Lender shall promptly remit to Participant, in the manner provided in paragraph 11 hereof: (1) the interest owing Participant on its participation in the Loan, as and when interest on the Loan is collected by Lender, (2) the Percentage of all other payments, avails and proceeds received by the Lender from any source pertaining to the Loan, including collateral and all sums realized from any endorser, guarantor or other person liable with respect to the Loan or from the exercise by Lender of any lien or right of set-off with respect to any deposit balance or other property of Borrower or other person liable with respect to the Loan. Interest on Participant's participation shall be payable at the rate of _____ % per annum on its undivided interest in the Loan notwithstanding that interest may be payable by the Borrower on the Loan at a higher rate.

5. Lender further represents and warrants to Participant that:

(a) Lender (or the Lead Bank) has not declared any default under the Loan or advised Borrower of any default and, to the best of Lender's knowledge, Borrower is not in default under any of the documents described in paragraph 2 hereof nor has it been in default prior to the date hereof;

(b) Lender has the full power and authority to enter into this agreement and complete the transactions contemplated hereby, and the representative of Lender executing this agreement is duly authorized to execute and deliver this agreement;

(c) Lender has itself, or has caused its duly authorized agent, to inspect the Improvements during the construction thereof, and Lender is not aware of any facts which would lead it to believe that the Improvements will not be completed on or before the expiration date of the Permanent Commitment or before the date on which any significant tenant of any material portion of the Improvements may cancel its lease because the Improvements have not been so completed; Lender is not aware of any facts which would cause it to believe that the undisbursed portion of the Loan will not be sufficient to complete the Improvements in accordance with the plans and specifications described on Schedule "A" and in accordance with the requirements of the Permanent Commitment; all of the conditions of the Permanent Commitment for closing thereunder have been complied with other than completion of the Improvements and conditions which cannot be complied with prior to such completion and the closing of the loan to be made pursuant to the Permanent Commitment.

6. Neither Lender nor Participant shall sell or otherwise dispose of all or any part of its respective interest in the Loan without the prior written approval of the other.

7. Lender agrees to notify Participant promptly of any default or other matter which may materially affect the interest of Participant in the Loan. Lender shall provide Participant with a monthly status report concerning the Loan and the amounts advanced and remaining to be advanced thereunder and the progress of the construction of the Improvements. Lender further shall mark its books to show the sale of a portion of its interest in the Loan to Participant hereunder so that the financial statements and other records of Lender will show as its interest in the Loan only such percentage thereof as has not been sold by it to Participant hereunder.

8. If Lender or the Lead Bank is to make any payments to third persons to protect the security of the Loan (such as taxes, insurance premiums, prior mortgage charges or rent) Lender shall advise Participant not less than 48 hours to the time such payments are to be made, and Participant shall pay to Lender the Percentage of such payments, and Lender and/or the Lead Bank shall pay the balance thereof; after each such Payment Lender shall furnish to Participant evidence of such payment.

9. In case of default by Borrower, Lender shall at once notify Participant in writing and, unless Participant shall otherwise consent, exercise (or cause the Lead Bank to exercise) the remedies available under the documents described in paragraph 2. After payment of all reasonable costs and expenses of foreclosure and collection, Lender shall promptly remit to Participant, Participant's proportionate share of all net proceeds received by Lender as a consequence of such foreclosure proceeding, including, without limiting the generality of the foregoing, proceeds of foreclosure sale, income from operation of the property pending liquidation, and proceeds of any resale.

10. Lender shall keep complete and accurate books, files and records of all matters pertaining to the Loan and make the same available for inspection by Participant or its authorized representative at any reasonable time.

11. Unless and until Participant shall otherwise advise Lender in writing, all payments shall be made by crediting Participant's account at,   , and notices, reports and documents shall be mailed or delivered to Participant's Manager,   . Notices to Lender by Participant shall be mailed or delivered to Lender at its address above set forth, or to such other address as Lender shall specify by notice, mailed or delivered as provided in the preceding sentence.

12. This agreement shall be governed by the Laws of   and shall not be binding unless and until executed and accepted by Participant.

13. Lender or Lead Bank shall service the Loan as an independent contractor and shall use its own equipment and employees and shall proceed by such means and in such manner as deemed best to carry out the terms of this agreement.

14. In the event of any material breach of any agreement by Lender herein or in the event that any representation or warranty of Lender herein shall be incorrect in any material respect, Lender shall, at Participant's option, repurchase Participant's participation in the Loan for the full amount of the purchase price paid by Participant (unless some portion thereof has prior

thereto been repaid in which event, the principal balance of Participant's share), together with interest at the rate to Participant provided herein from the dates of the disbursement of such purchase price to the date of such repurchase.

15. In case of any breach by the Lender in any agreement relating to the Loan or any failure of Lender or any other participant to make future advances on the Loan, the Participant shall, in addition to all other remedies available to it at law or in equity, have the right (but not the obligation) to purchase the interest in the Loan of the defaulting party at par plus accrued interest.

IN WITNESS WHEREOF, the parties hereto have caused these presents to be executed by their duly authorized officers and their respective seals to be affixed as of the day and year first above written.

By _____
(lender)

By _____
(participant)

SCHEDULE "A"

1. Name of Borrower.

2. Names of Guarantors, and purposes of guarantees.

3. Description of loan documents, including dates thereof, the parties thereto and recording data, if any.

4. Legal or other descriptions of the Property.

5. Description of Improvements.

6. Principal amount of the Loan, interest rate, and terms of payment of principal and interest.

7. Description of Permanent Commitment and buy-sell agreement (including name of issuer, loan amount and expiration date.)

8. Name of surety company issuing completion or performance and payment bond(s) and number of bond(s).

9. Name of company or companies issuing title insurance policy, number of policy and date and redate of issue, with names of reinsurer(s), if any, and the amount(s) reinsured.

10. Name of inspecting architect and date of last certification.

11. Name of insurance company or companies issuing builder's risk insurance policy, amount thereof and policy number.

12. Name of appraiser and date and amount of appraisal.

13. Description of plans and specifications of Improvements.

14. Name of surveyor of Property and last date to which survey has been updated.

15. Name of general contractor, date of construction contract and the completion date specified therein.

16. Name of the Lead Bank if other than the Lender.

RIDER A ATTACHED TO AND HEREBY MADE PART OF THAT CERTAIN PARTICIPATION AGREEMENT BETWEEN   AND DATED

The architect referred to in #10 of Schedule A shall be an independent architect whose qualifications are to be submitted to and approved by Participant prior to the execution of this agreement.

Before the funding of the first draw, there shall be submitted for approval of Participant:

(a) A schedule of values or an equivalent detailed cost breakdown by items;
(b) A full disclosure of the items to be paid for in the first draw, including indirect costs and the cost of work in place; and
(c) The lead lender's certified statement as to the source and availability of all funds required to complete the improvements over and above the construction loan proceeds.

Not later than seven business days prior to each succeeding draw, commencing with the third draw, Participant is also to receive and approve for the last draw a bringdown of the items set forth in "(a)" and "(b)" of the preceding paragraph.

Participant reserves the right to call for compliance with such requirements as its counsel may deem necessary with respect to any draws subsequent to the execution of this agreement.

NO. _____

PARTICIPATION CERTIFICATE

MORTGAGOR:

PROJECT AND LOCATION:

PARTICIPATION AGREEMENT DATED:

    THIS CERTIFIES that _____ has purchased a participation in the amount of _____, received by the undersigned on _____, in an advance made to mortgagor in the amount of _____ on _____; further that _____ now holds a total participation of _____ and that the undisbursed loan amounts to _____ as of the date hereof.

    THIS PARTICIPATION CERTIFICATE is issued in accordance with and subject to the terms and conditions of the Participation Agreement between the undersigned and _____ dated _____.

    ALL PARTICIPATION CERTIFICATES heretofore issued by the undersigned to _____ with reference to the mortgage for the above are superseded by this Certificate and of no further effect, it being the intent of this Participation Certificate to evidence the interest of _____ in the disbursements on account of said mortgage loan made by the undersigned to date.

_____

Attest: _____ By: _____

Date: _____

5
The Construction Loan Commitment

A SAMPLE COMMITMENT

After all of the loan underwriting has been completed, the loan has been structured to the parties' satisfaction and the basic business terms have been agreed upon, the lender should be prepared to issue its construction loan commitment. This commitment can take several forms as reflected upon in the following section.

A SAMPLE CONSTRUCTION LOAN COMMITMENT*

Construction loan commitments can, at one extreme, be brief, one-page letter agreements that set forth the bare essentials of the commitment, or they can be detailed documents that specify all the requirements that the borrower must satisfy before it can receive the loan proceeds. Of course, some commitments are neither brief nor fully detailed, and they fall somewhere between those two extremes.

"Bare Essentials" Commitments. "Bare essentials" commitments have the advantage of being simple and concise, and, therefore, of being readily acceptable to most borrowers. Such commitments usually set forth the names of the borrower and any guarantors, the loan amount, the interest rate, and any fees that the borrower must pay the lender. They describe briefly the security and the conditions upon

---

*This section, written by the author, is reprinted by permission from the *Real Estate Review,* Vol. 10, No. 4, Winter 1981, Copyright © 1981, Warren, Gorham and Lamont Inc., 210 South Street, Boston, Mass. All Rights Reserved.

which the lender is obligated to fund. They usually include the condition that "loan documents (like the building loan agreement, note and mortgage) will have to be acceptable to the lender in all respects."

A disadvantage of a bare essentials commitment is that it leaves room for misunderstandings at a later date. Despite the cautionary clause that the loan documents must be acceptable to the lender, the lender and borrower may have different ideas about the continuing conditions for funding the loan. When negotiations about those loan documents take place, the borrower may not wish to accept all the lender's documentation requirements, and the lender may find itself with an accepted commitment but no loan. Misunderstandings and disagreements that were papered over or ignored when a bare essentials commitment was executed usually emerge as the parties try to close the loan. In order to avoid this unhappy development, the lender who makes such a commitment should have a well-drafted building loan agreement ready to send to the borrower as soon as the borrower accepts the commitment. Thus the borrower will become aware of the lender's requirements at an early date.

"Detailed" Commitments. "Detailed" commitments have the advantage of resolving most, if not all, of the foreseeable misunderstandings and disagreements between the lender and the borrower at the outset of the negotiation. The borrower who receives such a commitment is fully aware of the lender's requirements and can work toward satisfying those requirements in a timely manner. If the borrower objects to any of the lender's requirements, he can make those objections known during the commitment stage rather than introducing them into the negotiation when the loan is otherwise ready to be closed. Consequently, delays at the time of loan closings are kept to a minimum.

The disadvantage of the "detailed" commitment is that its length and complexity may discourage some would-be borrowers. When a lender confronts its borrowers at the outset with numerous requirements and conditions, borrowers may come to the mistaken conclusion that the lender is overly demanding and inflexible. A lender that develops good personal relations with its borrowers may be able to remedy this situation. But sometimes it may lose the loan before it can establish a personal relationship. Critics of the "detailed" commitment take the position that an accepted commitment (even one that contains the possibility of future problems) is better than no commitment at all.

Moderately Detailed Commitments. Moderately detailed commitments, at first glance, appear to be a perfect compromise between the other two forms of commitments. They contain more information than "bare essentials" commitments, but they avoid the countless clauses of "detailed" commitments. Unfortunately, these characteristics may create more confusion and misunderstandings than the other two kinds of commitments combined. A commitment that tries to include some details loses the advantage of brevity, while it misleads the participants in a deal into believing that it resolves all foreseeable problems at the outset.

A Sample "Detailed" Commitment. Appended to this chapter is a good example of a "detailed" commitment. The first page of the example commitment sets forth the basic data of the transaction. This information would be included in any commitment whether "moderately detailed" or even "bare essentials." However, the fourteen paragraphs and many subparagraphs that comprise the "General Conditions of Construction Loan" describe in detail the lender's general loan requirements and makes this a "detailed commitment." To these "General Conditions," the negotiating parties may add a section entitled "Specific Conditions of Construction Loan" that describes any special agreements relating to the specific loan. These special conditions are not included in the example commitment.

The "General Conditions" start off by specifying the lender's insistence that it receive a first lien on the property and improvements and by listing the documents that must be executed by the parties. One of these documents is a building loan agreement that will govern the relationship between the parties throughout the construction period. Specifically, the "General Conditions" set forth conditions that the borrower must satisfy before the lender is obligated to disburse any construction loan advances. Specific data or evidence or documents that the borrower must supply before the lender will make the first advance, are listed in twenty subparagraphs to paragraph 4 of the General Conditions. Most of these borrower obligations are selfexplanatory; however, we would like to emphasize some and elaborate on others.

Appraisal Requirement. Paragraph 4(a) specifies that the qualified loan amount shall not exceed 75 percent of the project value established by an outside appraisal. The construction lender seeks this limitation because many permanent lenders, particularly life insurance companies, will not lend more than 75 percent of appraised value. A construction lender will advance more than this amount only if it is willing to take a second position for such excess funds when the permanent loan closes.

Submission of Plans and Specifications. It is of the utmost importance for the construction lender to obtain the approval of all the various loan parties (the permanent lender, the guarantors, the borrower, inspecting architect, etc.) to the final detailed plans and specifications of the project. Paragraph 4(c) specifies that the borrower submit these plans together with required approvals. The permanent lender will undoubtedly require, as a condition to disbursement of the permanent loan, that the completed improvements be in accordance with plans and specifications that the permanent lender has approved. The permanent commitment always includes the requirement that the completed improvements comply with all applicable governmental laws and regulations. Although the construction lender cannot, prior to the first advance, assure itself that these postconstruction requirements will be fulfilled, it can obtain whatever certifications and approvals are available at the time of construction loan closing.

Submission of Cost Breakdown. The basis of construction loan advances is an accurate breakdown of all costs of the proposed construction. Paragraph 4(e) requires the borrower to submit such a breakdown.

These data also make it possible for the lender to establish how much equity capital the developer needs in addition to the construction loan proceeds in order to complete the improvements. Since the inspecting architect will be monitoring the progress of construction relative to the lender's future advances, the borrower must submit evidence of that architect's approval of the submitted cost breakdown.

Submission of Financial Statements. Paragraph 4(f) requires the borrower to submit satisfactory financial statements that assure the lender that the various parties to the loan have the financial capacity to complete the project, even in the event of unforeseen delays or cost overruns.

Submission of Construction Contracts. Paragraph 4(h) instructs the borrower to submit various construction contracts to the lender for the latter's approval and to assign these contracts in order to protect the lender in the event that the borrower defaults on the loan and makes it necessary for the lender to step in and complete the project. Assignment of the contracts to the lender also serves the purpose of preventing any contract changes without the lender's consent. Any such changes could serve to exonerate a surety from liability or make the contract unacceptable to the lender should it have to perform thereunder.

Title Insurance. The mortgagee's policy of title insurance that paragraph 4(k) requires the borrower to provide for the construction lender should give the latter adequate protection against third parties claiming an interest in the land and should protect the lender against any mechanic's or materialmen's liens. The assignability of the policy to a permanent lender ensures that the same coverage will be available to the permanent lender.

Required Survey. The lender's need for the survey called for by paragraph 4(l) is obvious. To protect itself in the event the survey proves erroneous, the lender should insist that the survey's certification run to it. The lender should also require an updated survey at the time the foundation is completed. This foundation survey should establish that the improvements are being constructed within the property lines and any setback lines, and that there should be no encroachments onto or over known easements.

If this survey produces no evidence of problems, no additional surveys should be required until the project is completed.

Evidence of Land Purchase. The evidence of land purchase that paragraph 4(p) requires the borrower to submit is not necessary if the first advance is intended to include the acquisition cost of the land and the parties intend that there should be a simultaneous land purchase and mortgage closing.

Assignment of Permanent Commitment. The assignment of the permanent commitment and acknowledgment of the assignment by the permanent lender that paragraph 4(q) requires the borrower to obtain are necessary in order to assure the construction lender that the permanent commitment will not be amended or modified without the construction lender's consent. Absent such assignment and acknowledgement, a major amendment or modification of the permanent commitment could relieve the permanent lender of its permanent loan obligations and thus eliminate the intended source of repayment of the construction loan when the project is completed.

Evidence Relating to the Permanent Commitment. The protection of the permanent commitment as a source of funds for repayment of the construction loan is illustrated once again by the construction lender's requirements in paragraph 4(r). The construction lender must do everything possible to ensure that the permanent commitment is in full force and effect and will remain so at the time the project is completed. If this entails satisfying some of the permanent lender's requirements prior to the first advance even though the permanent lender will not call upon the borrower to meet these requirements until project completion (e.g., approval of tenant leases), so be it. The consequences of a defaulted permanent commitment could be disastrous for the construction lender.

Submission of Other Documents. The requirement in paragraph 4(t) that the borrower submit various other documents is basically a "catchall" that the lender may or may not need depending upon the specifics of the transaction. Sometimes the lender may permit the borrower to substitute a letter of credit for the performance bond. Such a letter of credit must usually be in an amount at least equal to an average advance. However, lenders permit such substitutions infrequently and only when the borrower advances convincing arguments why the bonding requirement should be waived.

Fees and Charges. Most construction lenders will require that the borrowers pay any fees or charges that were incurred in connection with the loan transaction. Examples of these charges are attorneys' fees, appraisal charges, architects' fees, etc. Paragraph 5 of the example commitment places the responsibility for these costs on the borrower. Paragraph 6 of the example commitment is basically boilerplate, a legal catchall, that should be included in all well-drafted commitments.

Completion Draft. Paragraph 7 reiterates the lender's concern that the improvements be completed in accordance with the approved plans and specifications. It also requires, among other things, that the improvements be completed at least thirty days prior to the maturity date of the note. This date should be tied into the termination date of the permanent loan commitment, with the thirty-day leeway giving the permanent lender sufficient time in which to inspect the completed improvements and close its loan.

Calculating Advances. Paragraph 8 sets forth the manner in which the amount of each construction advance is to be calculated. Other construction lenders may, of course, use methods that differ from those by the construction lender in the example commitment. The formula used in that document specifies that the lender will retain 10 percent of all construction costs, and it adds a safety factor to protect the lender in the event that the loan is "out of balance" (i.e., in the event the sum of the borrower's equity capital and the loan proceeds are not sufficient to meet total construction costs). If this should happen, the lender will not fund the full 90 percent of actual construction costs expended to date until the borrower comes up with sufficient additional equity capital. Although the wise lender writes such protection into its commitment, the probability that a well-underwritten loan will be "out of balance" is small unless interest rates skyrocket as they have done recently.

In paragraph 8, the formula for calculating the amount of advances does not differentiate between "hard" (actual construction) costs and "soft" (interest, attorney's fees, etc.) costs. It is not unusual for a lender to retain 10 percent of the borrower's hard costs but to advance 100 percent of the soft costs. If *ABC* Lending Institution, the example lender, were to agree to such terms, it would probably leave paragraph

8 stand as is, but it would make a special provision specifying a different retainage for soft costs, that would appear as part of the "Specific Conditions to Construction Loan."

Paragraph 8 limits the total amount to be disbursed by the lender to an amount not greater than the "Qualified Loan Amount." This term was first alluded to in paragraph 1 of the General Conditions. It is defined on the first page of the commitment as being "the amount qualified for disbursement under the permanent loan commitment, but in no event greater than the Maximum Loan Amount." The Maximum Loan Amount is a specific dollar amount that is listed on page 78. The reason that paragraph 8 limits the maximum amount that the lender will expend for construction is obvious. The construction lender does not want to be in a position where it has no assurance that funds will be available to pay off its entire loan when the project is completed. Of course, the Qualified Loan Amount may be increased during construction as and when the borrower meets various permanent lender requirements (e.g., rental achievement) for additional disbursements under the permanent loan commitment.

Materials Stored On-Site. Although our example loan commitment does not discuss the problem of funds for materials stored on-site, it is appropriate to discuss the problem at this point. It is quite common for borrowers to assert that once they have purchased and paid for materials and those materials are delivered to the site, the lender should be obliged to disburse the portion of the loan proceeds that was allocated to cover the cost of such materials. Lenders, on the other hand, are reluctant to advance any money for construction materials until those materials are actually in place. Materials stored on-site may be stolen or vandalized. If title to such materials is not fully vested in the borrower/developer, a creditor/materialman could easily repossess such materials. Developer/borrowers have been known to divert materials from one construction project to another. Accordingly, if the lender agrees to advance funds for materials stored on-site, it should condition fund disbursement upon its receipt of satisfactory evidence that the borrower owns the materials free and clear of any liens, that the materials are properly insured against theft and vandalism, and that adequate precaution or measures have been taken to safeguard the same. Again, conditions like these, if agreed to at the commitment stage of the transaction, should be set forth in the "Specific Conditions to Construction Loan."

Other Requirements. As construction work progresses, the borrower periodically requires the lender to release funds which the borrower needs to pay its contractors. To obtain each advance, the borrower must satisfy the lender that the loan is "in balance" and that construction completed to date has been in conformity with the approved plans and specifications. Paragraph 9 specifies that draw requests be submitted in such form that the lender can satisfy itself that all its conditions have been met. The lender's forms mentioned in paragraph 9 should call for all the information that the lender requires in order to determine whether its prerequisites for a construction loan advance have been satisfied.

The balance of the general conditions provide the lender with additional protections. Paragraph 12 prohibits informal amendments of the commitment and prevents the borrower from assigning it. Paragraph 14 provides a cut-off date for closing the loan transaction.

Specific Conditions of Construction Loan. As previously indicated, the specific conditions are usually arrived at as the result of specific agreements, or they arise in special circumstances. In some loan transactions, these special matters may be quite extensive; in others they may be nonexistent. The topics that are frequently the subject of specific conditions are methods of disbursement (i.e., via the title insurer or directly to the borrower), retainage, funding for materials stored on-site, bonding, and the manner in which the borrower is to furnish its equity capital (e.g., directly into the project or with a letter of credit).

THE AMENDMENT PROCESS

It is a rare situation where the lenders' commitment is sent to the borrower and unconditionally accepted. There are just too many possibilities for misunderstandings between the parties and differing positions on issues important to each for the lender to get it 100% right the first time around. What will usually occur is that the borrower will accept the commitment subject to certain modifications. The lender will then respond to this conditional acceptance either by issuing a revised commitment or an amendment to the original commitment. This, in turn, either will be accepted unconditionally by the borrower or further changes requested, once again eliciting a response from the lender. This procedure will continue until the final form of the commitment is agreed to (as is usually the case) or one or both parties give up trying to reach an accommodation.

Guarantees

One of the most important areas that lends itself to misunderstanding involves the issue of personal guarantees. Generally, the developer will agree to personally guarantee repayment of the loan and completion of construction. The lender often assumes that the borrowing entity will be similarly liable and draft its commitment accordingly. Objections may then be raised that for various reasons, the loan to the actual borrowing entity should be nonrecourse. In these circumstances, the developer may argue that a separate individual guarantee by the developer should satisfy the lender that the developer will not walk away from the project if problems arise. Lenders will generally concede to the borrower's request. However, the decision to exculpate the borrowing entity from personal liability while maintaining the right to go after the developer individually may have certain drawbacks, particularly should the borrowing entity be a partnership. For example, should a project encounter difficulties, the general partner/ developer who is personally liable may be willing to grant the lender certain concessions for release of his guarantee. These concessions may include deeding the property to the lender or remaining passive in a foreclosure action (see chapter 10). Other general partners and/or limited partners who object to the general partner/developer's conciliation could possibly take steps under the partnership agreement to block delivery of the deed to the lender or attempt to assert themselves as interested parties in the foreclosure proceedings. This latter tactic could be done with impunity since the loan to the partnership is nonrecourse. The solution for the lender is to require that all general partners join in the guarantee or be limited in their rights to a say on future workouts and to insist that the partnership agreement restrict the rights of any limited partners in work-out type situations.

Lender Approvals

A major area of contention between the lenders and borrowers involves the various approvals needed from the lender called for throughout the commitment. In lieu of establishing specific objective standards for granting approvals, the borrower will often attempt to condition the lender's approvals by requiring them "not to be unreasonably withheld." No one knows for certain what these words mean, other than the fact that they are invitations to a lawsuit should a dispute arise. For this reason and simply because the lender desires the commitment to be as favorable to it as possible, most lenders will object strenuously to conditioning their consent in this manner.

Fast Track Construction

The Commitment requirement for final plans and specifications to be submitted prior to the first advance will cause borrowers a problem if they are attempting a "fast track" method of construction whereby the plans and specifications are formulated as construction progresses on a stage by stage basis. Developers can achieve significant cost savings by utilizing this approach and lenders may consider waiving the requirements for the receipt of final plans and specifications provided: (1) they are dealing with a developer who has a proven track record and substantial net worth, (2) the foundation permit has been issued and the foundation plans have been accepted by the city wherein the property is located, (3) the provider of take-out financing has approved the fast track approach and (4) provision is contained in the loan documents for the lender to receive, prior to the commencement of any new stage of construction, approvals from the applicable governmental authorities and provider of take-out financing for the stage of construction just completed and plans and specifications together with firm construction contracts for the next stage of construction to be undertaken.

Calculating Advances

The lender's method of calculating advances is another area to which borrowers often take exception. There is no objection to lenders holding back retainage, but borrowers would like this retainage released as soon as possible. Requests for the retainage to be released for each subcontractor after its work is completed or for all retainage to be released when 50% of the project is completed are commonplace. This is not to say though that they are readily granted by the lender. Some construction lenders insist that the retainage will not be released until final completion, not even tempering their position with reference to "substantial completion." Other lenders are more liberal and will readily release the retainage upon request. Perhaps a good compromise would be for the retainage to be held back only until 50% of the project is completed, with such retainage not being released until substantial completion of the entire project. Alternately, a lender can feel fairly comfortable if it releases retainage with regard to a particular trade, but only if all work to be done for the project by the trade has been satisfactorily completed. Of course, any concessions by the lender regarding retainage should be conditioned upon the loan being "in balance" and free from default and any statutory requirements for retainage complied with. However, in those states where retainage of the final payment is required (e.g., Florida), there is little incentive for the lender to release its retainage and there is a risk that it may not be maintained by the borrower or general contractor.

Conclusion

Other general conditions of the commitment and/or the special conditions could give rise to requested commitment changes. The extent of these requests and the changes actually made will depend upon the specific nature of the transaction, the degree of prior negotiations and the relationship between the parties. A borrower and lender who have worked well together in the past and are familiar with each other's procedures should be able to finalize a commitment in short order. When no prior relationship exists, each party will most likely seek clarification of the other's methods and intentions, thereby prolonging the commitment process.

APPENDIX

SAMPLE DETAILED COMMITMENT

ABC Construction Lending Institution

COMMITMENT TO:
Date:
To:

This constitutes a commitment of *ABC* Construction Lending Institution (hereinafter referred to as *ABC*) to make a construction mortgage loan to the Borrower subject to the specific terms hereinafter set forth, to the "General Conditions of Construction Loan" and to "Specific Conditions of Construction Loan" annexed hereto and made a part hereof:

Borrower(s):

Property and Improvements:

Qualified Loan Amount: The amount qualified for disbursement under the permanent loan commitment, but in no event greater than the Maximum Loan Amount.

Maximum Loan Amount: $

Permanent Loan Commitment: Commitment No.   dated

Permanent Lender:

Variable Interest Rate:

Maturity Date:

Guarantor(s):

Nonrefundable Commitment Fee: $

Inspecting Architect:

ABC Counsel:

Loan Officer:

This commitment shall be considered null and void unless you indicate your acceptance by signing and returning the attached copy of this commitment to us together with the Nonrefundable Commitment Fee in care of the Loan Officer by no later than

By: *ABC* Construction Lending Institution

AGREED TO AND ACCEPTED
THIS .... day of .... 19....
....
....
....

GENERAL CONDITIONS OF CONSTRUCTION LOAN

ABC COMMITMENT NO. ....

Date: ....

(1) The construction mortgage loan contemplated by this commitment to the Borrower shall be secured at all times by a first lien on the Property and Improvements and shall be in an amount not to exceed the Qualified Loan Amount.

(2) This commitment and our obligation to make advances under the loan are subject to satisfaction of the terms hereof and to the Permanent Loan Commitment being in full force and effect at all times throughout the term of our loan.

(3) The loan is to be evidenced by the Borrower's promissory note for the Maximum Loan Amount which shall bear a variable Interest Rate payable monthly and be due and payable in full at the Maturity Date and is to be secured by a mortgage which shall be a first lien on the fee simple title to the security with any ground lease or leases expressly subordinated, and additionally secured by (i) security agreements and financing statements creating a first lien covering all supplies delivered and to be used in the construction of the Improvements to be financed hereby as well as all equipment and furnishings actually installed in the Improvements; it is understood and agreed that the inclusion of any and all non-fixture items is solely for the purpose of insuring completion of construction and compliance with the Permanent Loan Commitment and not for the purpose of producing income or return on investment; (ii) an assignment of rents and leases free of any prior interest in said rents and leases; (iii) a building loan agreement; (iv) the unconditional joint and several guaranty by the Guarantors of completion of construction and of repayment of the indebtedness; and (v) such other documents as are designated by ABC's Counsel (all hereinafter collectively referred to as the Loan Documents). The Loan Documents are to be satisfactory to us and our Counsel both as to form and content.

(4) The Improvements shall be constructed and the loan advanced in accordance with the terms of the building loan agreement, which, among other things, shall require the inspection of construction and approval of advances (to be made not more frequently than once monthly) by the Inspecting Architect, and the receipt and approval by

us and our Counsel both as to form and content prior to the first advance (the initial closing) of the following:
- (a) An appraisal, also to be approved by the Permanent Lender, prepared without cost to us by an appraiser acceptable to us and the Permanent Lender. The Qualified Loan Amount shall in no event exceed 75 percent of the value established by such appraisal;
- (b) The undertakings of the general contractor, architect and engineer, if any, to continue performance on our behalf without additional cost in the event of a default under any of the loan documents;
- (c) One set of final detailed plans and specifications for all construction, including borings and soil reports and evidence of permanent lender's acceptance thereof, designating the manufacturer and model number of all equipment (i) with the approval of the Borrower, Guarantors, Permanent Lender and Inspecting Architect noted thereon; (ii) bearing an endorsement by the appraiser that he has examined said plans and specifications and finds them to be in keeping with the basis on which he appraised the property for us; (iii) accompanied by a certification by an architect acceptable to us that the plans and specifications meet all applicable local zoning, building and other pertinent requirements of the public authorities having jurisdiction, including, but not limited to, compliance with the National Environmental Policy Act and any other applicable federal, state, municipal or local environmental impact or energy laws or regulations, and that the construction covered thereby is sound, of good design and satisfactory for the purpose intended; (iv) accompanied by a certification by a qualified professional engineer acceptable to us certifying on a basis of personal inspection, with supporting data (borings, soil reports, etc.) that what is planned and specified will be adequate, and (v) showing that the parking facilities will be constructed as required within the security. Any and all changes from the approved plans and specifications must be approved by us;
- (d) The Loan Documents executed by all parties necessary to create the rights and duties respectively set out in each document;
- (e) A detailed cost breakdown showing all costs of the proposed

construction with the approval of the Inspecting Architect that the cost breakdown is reasonable and accurate being noted thereon;
(f) Current financial statements for the Borrower, Guarantors, general contractor and major subcontractors;
(g) Evidence that the Property is free and clear of all restrictions and encumbrances unless approved by us;
(h) Architects', contractors', subcontractors' and engineers' contracts relating to construction of the Improvements with parties acceptable to us and assignments of said contracts to us;
(i) Borrower's affidavit and opinion of Borrower's Counsel;
(j) Form lease to be used for all tenants;
(k) A policy of mortgagee's title insurance written by a title company or companies acceptable to us on the American Land Title Association 1970 Loan Policy form assignable to a permanent mortgagee;
(l) A current survey certified to us and the title insurer; a foundation survey will also be required when the foundation is completed and we reserve the right to call for interim surveys locating the improvements as construction progresses;
(m) Evidence of compliance with all laws, ordinances, rules, regulations and restrictions affecting the premises, the construction of the improvements and the consummation of the transaction, including but not limited to zoning, issuance of all building permits and licenses and availability of utility and municipal services;
(n) Such policies of builder's risk, liability, workmen's compensation and other insurance as we may require in forms, companies and amounts acceptable to us, including, but not limited to, collapse insurance;
(o) Evidence that sufficient funds have been made available by the Borrower in a manner satisfactory to us for the purpose of completing the improvements heretofore described;
(p) Evidence that the Borrower has purchased the land herein referred to and has fully paid for it;
(q) An assignment of the Borrower's rights under the Permanent Loan Commitment, with such assignment approved by the Permanent Lender;
(r) Evidence that all requirements of the Permanent Loan Com-

mitment which can be satisfied prior to the initial closing have been complied with to the satisfaction of the Permanent Lender, including but not limited to approval by the Permanent Lender of the state of title and survey; that the Permanent Loan Commitment is in full force and effect, without modification, except as we may have approved in writing, and that the Permanent Lender has agreed to accept the certificate of the Inspecting Architect in satisfaction of any conditions of the Permanent Loan Commitment requiring certification as to performance of construction and completion of improvements in accordance with the plans and specifications;

(s) Evidence as to the Borrower's capacity and authority to take the loan and to execute the Loan Documents;

(t) Such other documents, instruments, opinions, and assurances as we may require including but not limited to 100 percent labor and material payment and performance bonds covering the general contractor and/or subcontractors in amounts and issued by companies satisfactory to us, in which we are to be named as dual obligee, assignments of specified leases and, at our option, an agreement by the Permanent Lender for the purchase of the note and mortgage;

(5) The loan shall be made without cost to us. The fees of our Counsel, the appraiser, the Inspecting Architect, title insurance premiums and charges, survey charges, mortgage and documentary stamp taxes, if any, recording charges, brokerage commissions and any other connected costs shall be payable by the Borrower and the Guarantors, and the Borrower and the Guarantors hereby jointly and severally agree to pay such fees and to indemnify us against claims of brokers arising in connection with the execution of this commitment by us or the consummation of the loan contemplated hereby, all regardless of whether the loan contemplated hereby closes.

(6) Our Counsel shall be satisfied that all fees and charges respecting the making of the loan will result in no exceeding of any applicable interest limitation of the jurisdiction in which the property securing the loan is located. The loan and our making of it shall be in all respects legal and shall not violate any applicable law or other requirement of any governmental authority.

(7) The improvements are to be constructed in accordance with the approved appraisal and final plans and specifications, and are to be completed, free of all liens, other than the lien of the construction mortgage contemplated hereby, not less than thirty days in advance of the Maturity Date of the Note.

(8) The proceeds of the loan shall be advanced (a) as construction progresses, but not more frequently than once a month, in amounts which at our election shall be 90 percent of either:

(a) The amount of the qualified loan multiplied by the percentage of completion of construction then attained; or
(b) The estimated total cost of construction of the improvements as determined at the time of each advance by the Inspecting Architect, (and/or, at our option, by our in-house architect) multiplied by the percentage of completion of construction then attained, less the difference between said estimated total cost of construction and the amount of the qualified loan.

less in each case, amounts theretofore advanced; and (b) in no event in an amount greater than the Qualified Loan Amount. Funds will be advanced for materials stored on-site only at our option.

(9) Each request for funds from the Borrower shall be on *ABC*'s forms, duly approved for payment by the Contractor, Inspecting Architect and Borrower and accompanied by all documentation deemed necessary by us to substantiate the requested payment. Draw requests are to be sent to the Loan Officer in sufficient time to allow five (5) business days for processing and wiring of funds.

(10) By accepting this commitment, the Borrower agrees, at our request, to affix a sign approved by us, at a location on the premises satisfactory to us, which shall recite, among other things, that *ABC* is financing the construction.

(11) This commitment assumes the accuracy of all information, representations, exhibits and other matter submitted to us and presupposes no material adverse change in the state of facts indicated therein prior to any disbursement of funds hereunder.

(12) This commitment may be amended only by a writing executed by us and is not assignable without our prior written consent.

(13) After accepting this commitment, the Borrower is requested to

promptly get in touch with our Counsel for the purpose of arranging for the preparation of the Loan Documents and other items necessary for the initial closing.

(14) The initial closing shall be held on a date within 45 days from the date of the acceptance of this commitment, upon not less than five days written notice to us, care of the Loan Officer. No such notice shall be effective to establish a closing date unless we shall have previously received and approved a current report of title and the requisite survey. Unless the initial closing is held within such 45-day period, our obligation hereunder will, at our option, terminate.

6
Preparation for Loan Closing

LEGAL REQUIREMENTS

Once the commitment has been accepted, the loan underwriter will request that the lender's attorney commence preparation for the loan closing. By this time the attorney should be familiar with the transaction and be in a position to draft the requisite loan documents. At the time of such preparation, the lender's attorney should advise all parties of what documents are needed and coordinate the furnishing and acceptance of all outstanding items. A more detailed discussion of the role of the construction lender's attorney is contained in the following section:

A CHECKLIST FOR THE CONSTRUCTION LENDER'S ATTORNEY*

Once a construction lender has issued its commitment for construction financing, an enormous number of documents must flow between lender and borrower. The "checklist" that is appended to this article includes seventeen documents that must be prepared by lender's attorney, eight documents that borrower's attorney must submit to lender, and twenty other types of documents (appraisals, plans, certifications, leases, etc.) that the borrower must obtain for the lender.

---

*This section, written by the author, is reprinted by permission from the *Real Estate Review*, Vol. 11, No. 4, Winter 1982, Copyright © 1982, Warren, Gorham and Lamont Inc., 210 South Street, Boston, Mass. All Rights Reserved.

86 A PRACTICAL GUIDE TO CONSTRUCTION LENDING

Although the checklist is generally complete, it is by no means adequate for every possible transaction. Particular transactions may require documents that are not listed in the checklist and the checklist may include documents that are not needed for certain transactions. Nevertheless, counsel for both parties, the lender's underwriter, and the borrower's principals should all be aware of the documents that must be obtained and exchanged in the complex transaction known as a construction loan.

In the paragraphs that follow, we make brief comments about each of the checklisted items.

Loan Documents Prepared by Lender's Counsel. In order to expedite closing, the construction lender's counsel should prepare the loan documents enumerated below as soon as the borrower accepts the lender's commitment. These documents should be forwarded not only to the borrower's counsel, but, if a buy-sell agreement is contemplated among the construction lender, the take-out or long-term lender and the borrower, the documents should also be sent to permanent lender's counsel for review and comments.

Promissory Note. The promissory note is a fairly standard document, and it usually is not the cause of contention between the parties. Occasionally, the borrower's counsel may seek certain notice and grace periods in connection with the payment of interest. However, such requests are usually not appropriate in a construction loan in which the interest due is funded from the construction loan proceeds. However, notice and grace periods may become important should the borrower have to come up with additional funds in the event of cost overruns or the interest reserve runs out.

Mortgage or Deed of Trust. The mortgage or deed of trust is also usually a fairly standard document. The borrower's attorney will no doubt request "notice and an opportunity to cure" defaults as well as the right to apply any hazard insurance or condemnation proceeds toward restoration of the premises. The construction lender must be careful about the rights that it concedes here. Any extension periods or restoration provisions must be related to the commitment for permanent financing, and to the target date for completion of the improvements that is set forth in that commitment. For example, if the construction lender agrees in the mortgage document to apply the proceeds of a fire loss toward restoration of the property rather than toward payment of the indebtedness, it must reserve the right to refuse to permit this use of insurance proceeds if it believes that the damage has set back the construction time table so extensively that the permanent lender's completion date will not be met. In addition, the right to so apply the funds must be conditioned upon the funds being disbursed pursuant to the safeguards outlined in the Building (or Construction) Loan Agreement. This means that the borrower may be required to furnish additional equity capital should the lender deem that to be necessary.

Assignment of Rents/Assignment of Lessor's Interest. The assignment of rents and/or the assignment of lessor's interest is another fairly standard document. In most situations it is of little significance to the construction lender because the property will not be leased until after construction is completed. However, it can be extremely important if the property is preleased, if a buy-sell agreement is contemplated, if the permanent loan commitment requires that a rental achievement be met before the permanent lender will fund the long-term loan, or in the event construction is completed and the property leased, but for some reason the construction lender has to enforce its remedies under the loan documents.

Guaranty of Completion and Repayment. Generally, the construction loan commitment requires that one or more parties, other than the borrower, guaranty the completion of construction and/or repayment of the indebtedness. If more than one party is involved, the document should be drafted so that there is joint and several liability. The document should give the construction lender the right to proceed against the guarantors without first having to exhaust its remedies against the property and/or the borrower. There are usury implications in a guaranty to complete. If the guarantor's cost to complete is so high that the guarantor must expend a sum greater than the legal interest maximum, the lender may be subject to a usury charge. In such a case, the discharge of the debt should also discharge the obligation to complete.

Uniform Commercial Code (UCC) Financing Statements. The construction lender needs UCC financing statements in order to perfect its security interest in any personalty belonging to the borrower and pledged as security for the loan. The statements should specifically include as security any building materials that the borrower has purchased but has not yet installed as part of the premises. This language should be specific because there is a dispute in some jurisdictions as to whether such property may be presumed a construction loan security. The UCC financing statement should specify the lender's right to any hazard insurance or condemnation proceeds as well.

Security Agreement. Many construction lenders do not prepare a separate security agreement because it is common practice to incorporate special language in the mortgage or deed of trust, making those documents the security agreement and alluding to UCC remedies as being included.

UCC Lien Search. Lender's counsel should order a UCC lien search to ensure that the lender has a first priority security interest in the collateral covered by the UCC financing statements. Since it may take thirty days to receive the lien search, borrower's affidavits are often substituted for the searches at closing.

Disbursement Agreement. The manner in which the construction loan proceeds are to be advanced is usually set forth in the building (or construction) loan agreement, the capstone document in the construction loan transaction. However, some construction agreements specify that a disbursing agent (typically the title insurance company) is to be used. Since the disbursing agent is not a party to the building loan agreement, a separate disbursement agreement is necessary. The agreement should reiterate the lender's conditions in the building loan agreement for disbursements, and it should clearly define the obligations and responsibilities of the parties to the disbursement process.

Assignment of Construction Contracts. In order to be able to continue construction should the loan go into default, the lender should obtain an assignment of the borrower's rights in his contracts with the general contractor, major subcontractors, the architect, and the engineer.

The assignment of the borrower's rights in the contract with the architect should also include the borrower's rights to use the plans and specifications.

Consent to Assignment and Undertakings to Perform. The lender should also obtain the consent of the various parties to the construction contracts (general contractor, architect, etc) to the assignment of these contracts. The lender should obtain their written undertaking to perform on the lender's behalf pursuant to the terms of the original contract in the event the lender exercises its rights under the assignment and takes over the project. Most contractors will agree to this provided the lender agrees to make the progress payments called for by their contract. There is often a problem about the point at which the lender's responsibilities for the progress payments commence. The lender should always insist that, at take-over time, the borrower's unpaid bills are not its obligation.

Asssignment of Permanent Lender's Commitment. The construction lender usually looks to the permanent lender as the source of funds for repayment of its loan. Prior to committing its construction loan, the construction lender therefore carefully reviews the permanent loan commitment to ascertain that its requirements are reasonable and can be met in a timely manner. To ensure that the terms of the permanent loan commitment are not renegotiated without the construction lender's approval, the construction lender must obtain an assignment of the borrower's rights to the commitment. The permanent lender should consent to the assignment, although it may limit that consent to granting the construction lender the right to cure the borrower's defaults and to approve commitment changes. Permanent lenders do not usually agree to make their loan to the construction lender should the latter exercise its rights under the assignment. But it is worthwhile for the construction lender to attempt to obtain such agreement.

Buy-Sell or Tri-Party Agreement. An important document in any new construction arrangement is a buy-sell or tri-party agreement to which the parties are the construction lender, the permanent lender, and the borrower. This document calls for the construction lender to assign its loan to the permanent lender once the borrower has complied with the requirements for the permanent loan commitent, and places restrictions on modification of the construction loan documents during the course of construction and enforcement during default. Since this document benefits the permanent lender as well as the construction lender, its execution is often found as a requirement of both the permanent and construction loan commitments. The construction lender benefits because the document locks in the permanent loan commitment.

Letter of Assurances. Of more immediate importance to the construction lender than the buy-sell agreement is a letter of assurances from the permanent lender that says that the borrower has complied with the permanent loan commitment requirements. This letter should state that the permanent loan commitment is in full force and effect, that all fees due thereunder have been paid, and that all requirements which are capable of being satisfied at the time the construction loan closes have in fact been satisfied in a timely manner. It should also assert the permanent lender's approval of the plans and specifications, perimeter survey, existing title report, and any other documents relating specifically to the project (like a spur track agreement or management agreement).

The letter of assurances need not be a separate document; it may be included as part of the buy-sell or tri-party agreement.

Borrower's Affidavit. To assure the construction lender that the borrower has been truthful in its submissions for the loan, the construction lender should insist that the borrower sign an affidavit that asserts among other things that the borrower is a duly formed entity, that those signing on behalf of the borrower have authority to do so and that there are no outstanding judgments or present or threatened litigation against the borrower. The affidavit should be signed personally by a principal of the borrowing entity.

Opinion of Borrower's Counsel. Since the loan documents and the project itself must comply with various legal requirements, an Opinion of Borrower's Counsel is usually required. To ensure the construction lender that the opinion is as broad as possible, the initial draft should be prepared by the lender's counsel. Typically, such opinions cover the validity of the borrowing entity and its authority to enter into the loan, enforceability of the loan documents and compliance with zoning, usury, and ecological laws.

Building Loan Agreement. The basic terms governing the relationship between the borrower and construction lender during the course of construction are set forth in the building loan agreement (sometimes called the "construction loan agreement"). This is the chief document of the construction loan. It sets forth the requirements that the borrower must meet in order to qualify for construction advances, the manner in which such advances are to be calculated, and the method of their disbursement. Procedures governing construction delays and defaults are also included in this document as well as provisions relating to the application of hazard insurance proceeds and condemnation awards, among other things.

Loan Documents Submitted by Borrower's Counsel. The construction lender should ask borrower's counsel to submit the following documents as soon as the borrower accepts the construction lender's commitment, if it has not done so before that time.

Commitment for Title Insurance. The lender wants a Title Commitment in its favor issued by a title company that is acceptable to the lender and that will issue the final mortgagee's title policy. The title commitment should be accompanied by certified copies of all easements, restrictions, and other title exceptions that appear in the commitment. In addition, the legal description of land comprising the security should be identical to the description contained in the surveyor's certificate.

The construction lender should insist that a copy of the title commitment and accompanying documents should be sent promptly to the permanent lender's counsel. This will facilitate the permanent lender's execution of the letter of assurances previously referred to.

Recorded Plat. Borrower should submit a certified copy of the recorded plat showing the relative location of the surveyed land to the rest of the land in the same plat.

Survey. Together with the recorded plat, the borrower should submit a current certified survey of the security property that has been prepared by a registered professional engineer or a licensed public surveyor for the appropriate jurisdiction. The survey should set forth the dimensions of the land and its location with respect to all dedicated public streets and should clearly locate and identify, by reference to the volume and page where recorded, all easements and rights of way affecting the property. It should reflect the foundation lines laid, any building setback lines required by the local jurisdiction, contain a metes and bounds legal description of the land, and be certified to the lender, the borrower, and the title company by the public surveyor.

Documents Creating the Borrower. We indicated earlier that lender's counsel should prepare for the borrower's signature an affidavit that assures the lender that the borrower and the parties signing on behalf of the borrower have authority to enter into the transaction. The construction lender should further require the borrower to submit true and correct copies of the documents that created the borrowing entity and any amendments thereto. These documents may consist of articles of partnership or of incorporation, or a joint venture agreement or a land trust agreement or similar document.

Lease Form. The borrower should also submit to the construction lender the proposed standard form of tenant lease. Since a lender may one day become owner of the property through foreclosure, it must examine the lease through the eyes of a potential landlord.

Evidence of Availability of Utilities. In order for the project to be viable upon completion, all utilities (gas, electric, water and sewer, telephone) that are necessary to service the proposed building must be available at the property line. To evidence such availability, the borrower should send the lender copies of letters of current date from all local companies and/or municipal agencies that identify the real property involved and assure that adequate service for all legal occupants will be available at the property line when the structure is completed.

Building Permit. A prerequisite to any construction is the issuance by the local authority of a building permit for the building to be located on the security. The lender should advance no construction funds until the permit is obtained.

Verification of Zoning Compliance. Although the opinion of borrower's counsel should assert compliance with zoning regulations, the lender's counsel should require the borrower to submit written verification from the appropriate jurisdiction that such property is zoned under a classification that permits the construction of the proposed building for the proposed use, and that the building meets parking requirements if any are specified. If the jurisdiction has established no zoning or parking requirements, the written verification should confirm these facts.

Business Requirements. In addition to documents prepared by its own counsel and documents prepared by the borrower's counsel, the construction lender requires the borrower to submit a host of other documents that we have identified as "business documents." The borrower usually transmits these documents directly to the lender's loan underwriter. However, it may be wise, and it is sometimes necessary that the construction lender's attorney participate in expediting compliance with business requirements. Since these documents are prepared by professionals other than legal counsel, we will not comment on them in this article.

However, lender's counsel should carefully review the commitment and be familiar with the business documents that the commitment calls for. Although such items vary from commitment to commitment, the following checklist sets forth numerous business items typically called for in a construction loan. We remind the reader that any checklist can merely serve as a guide and may, for any specific transaction, be incomplete.

A CHECKLIST FOR THE CONSTRUCTION LENDER'S ATTORNEY

☐ Loan Documents to be Prepared by Lender's Counsel:
- Promissory note.
- Mortgage or deed of trust.
- Assignment of rents/assignment of lessor's interest.
- Guaranty of completion and repayment.

- UCC financing statements.
- Security agreement.
- UCC lien search.
- Disbursement agreement.
- Assignment of construction contracts and plans and specifications.
- Consent to assignment of contracts.
- Undertakings to perform.
- Assignment of permanent lender's commitment.
- Buy-sell or tri-party agreement.
- Letter of assurances.
- Borrower's affidavit.
- Opinion of borrower's counsel.
- Building loan agreement.

☐ Loan Documents to be Submitted by Borrower's Counsel:
- Title commitment.
- Recorded plat.
- Survey.
- Documents creating the borrowing entity (e.g., Official Certificate of Incorporation, etc., By-laws, Good Standing).
- Tenant lease form.
- Evidence of availability of utilities.
- Building permit.
- Verification of zoning and environmental compliance.

☐ Typical Business Requirements:
- Appraisal.
- Final plans and specifications with notations and approvals as required by commitment.
- Borings and soils reports.
- Permanent lender's approval of plans.
- Architect's certification of plan acceptability.
- Engineer's certification on foundations.
- Detailed cost breakdown.
- Architect's approval of cost breakdown.
- Current financial statements, borrower, guarantor, general contractor, major subcontractors.
- Foundation survey.
- Insurance policies (hazard and casualty).

- Statement of source of construction funds.
- Evidence of land purchase (title report).
- Signed copy of permanent loan commitment and any amendments.
- Signed contracts (manually executed counterparts) with general contractor, major subcontractors, architect, and engineer.
- Evidence of satisfied permanent loan commitment conditions (to the extent available).
- Labor and material payment bonds.
- Draw request (form).
- Signed leases, if any.
- Letter of credit or certificate of deposit, if required.

BUSINESS REQUIREMENTS

At the time the lender's attorney is required to commence preparation for the loan closing, the loan administrator will be asked to insure that all business requirements of the commitment will be satisfied prior to closing. A checklist of Typical Business Requirements is set forth at the end of the preceding section. This list is fairly indicative of the business requirements for most construction loans. However, it should *not* be taken as a definitive list for any particular loan. Such a list can only be prepared after a complete review of the lender's file and the loan commitment.

Forms

To expedite compliance with the business requirements, the loan administrator should alert the borrower to those matters which must be taken care of prior to loan closing. Lenders customarily have their own forms for this purpose and a standard form of notice letter (Exhibit A) with a copy of each of the forms referred to are attached at the end of this section. These forms, the typical business requirements not analyzed in previous chapters and the loan administrator's role in the compliance process will be the subject of the remainder of this chapter.

Appraisal

If an appraisal is called for by the commitment, the loan administrator should contact the designated appraiser and see to the submission of the appraisal within the time restraints of the commitment (usually within 30–60 days from the time the commitment was issued). He should also be satisfied that the final appraisal is based upon the approved plans and specifications which have been the basis (or are to be the basis) upon which building permits will be sought and that it is acceptable to the lender, confirming the basis upon which the loan was underwritten.

Final Plans and Specifications

The final plans and specifications should be submitted to the lender's architect/engineer accompanied by the certification attached as Exhibit B. The loan administrator must be assured that this has been accomplished, with the plans and specifications reviewed and all discrepancies resolved. The submitted final plans and specifications should also be reviewed and accepted by the inspecting architect, general contractor and the provider of take-out funds. A letter to the inspecting architect outlining the scope of his services and the inspecting architect's agreement are attached as Exhibits C and D.

Fast Track Construction. When a fast track method of construction is being utilized, there will be no final plans and specifications prior to loan closing. In this situation, preliminary plans and specifications should be received by the lender and the loan administrator should insure that the fast track procedure and the preliminary plans and specifications are acceptable to all concerned parties, particularly the provider of take-out funds. Needless to say, the loan administrator should set up a tickler system for receipt of the final plans and specifications and at such time, obtain the requisite approvals.

Borings and Soil Reports

The loan administrator's role regarding borings and soil reports is simply to insure that they have been submitted, reviewed and accepted by all appropriate parties; that is, the lender's architect/engineer, the inspecting architect and the provider of take-out funds. He should also verify that the engineer-of-record certification, attached as Exhibit E, is completed, and depending upon the degree of construction, that the engineered fill certification and foundation completion certification (Exhibits F and G) are also completed.

Detailed Cost Breakdown

The submitted cost breakdown must be carefully reviewed for accuracy and completeness. A form of cost breakdown is attached as Exhibit H. This is usually done by the lender's architect/engineer and the inspecting architect (a form of inspecting architect's cost certification is attached as Exhibit I). Based upon the cost estimate and the available funds from the construction loan, a determination must then be made as to the sufficiency of funds necessary for completion of the project. This determination should conform with the preliminary determination made during the loan underwriting process and should also be consistent with the borrower's statement as to the source of construction funds (Exhibit J).

Hazard and Casualty Insurance Policies

The hazard and casualty insurance policies received should be in amounts and issued by companies acceptable to the lender. Most large institutional lenders have separate departments that review these policies. However, before forwarding the policies to the appropriate parties for review, the loan administrator should first verify that the amounts are as required in the commitment and that a standard mortgagees clause is attached naming the lender as additional insured.

Labor and Material Payment and Performance Bonds

If labor and material payment and performance bonds are required by the commitment, the loan administrator must be sure they have been received and that they name the lender as co-obligee. Bonding is desirable to the construction lender for several reasons. The labor and material payment bond will guarantee payment to subcontractors and thus free the property from potential mechanics' liens. The performance bond guarantees the borrower and the lender that provided the contract payments are made, the surety will complete the work even if the contractor does not.

One of the problems faced by lenders when bonds are required stems from the fact that few, if any, sureties will bond an owner-builder. They insist that the builder be a totally independent contractor. The answer here is for the lender to require bonding of the major subcontractors rather than the related general contractor, although the bonding limits may not be as high as the lender would prefer. A more important problem is the sensitivity of bonds and the fact that a change in the transaction without the approval of the surety, may serve to exonerate the bonding company from liability. This places a burden on the loan administrator to keep the surety advised of any such changes and obtain the requisite consents when appropriate.

Draw Request

The attached from of application and certificate for payment (Exhibits H and K) should be submitted to the loan administrator prior to closing. This form doubles as the cost breakdown form and provides an ongoing basis for future draw requests. The loan administrator should be sure prior to authorizing disbursement that the loan is "in balance" and that the certifications by the contractor, inspecting architect and borrower set forth on the application and certificate for payment form have been completed.

Letter of Credit

If a letter of credit is to be received for balancing purposes or for any other reason, the construction lender should insist that it be unconditional and irrevocable. It should be available simply by the lender's draft(s) at sight and should contain no preconditions for disbursement. It should, however, contain an express waiver of any rights the issuing bank may have to defer or delay payment. Although banks may initially object to these requirements, most will ultimately concede to the lender's demands, particularly when it is brought to their attention that the letter of credit is being taken by the lender in lieu of cash as a courtesy to the borrower. If there are to be any disputes over the right to have lender's draft honored under the letter of credit, these should be between the lender and the borrower and not between the lender and the bank. A sample form of acceptable letter of credit is attached at the end of this chapter as Exhibit L.

Closing

When all of the business requirements have been satisfied, the loan administrator should notify the lender's attorney and when the legal requirements have been met, the loan is ready to be closed.

EXHIBIT A

TO: BORROWER
FROM: ABC CONSTRUCTION LENDING INSTITUTION

The ABC commitment recently issued for the referenced loan requires that specific certifications be made prior to loan closing. Accordingly, in an effort to assist you in complying with these requirements we are enclosing forms for distribution.

Prior to loan closing the following are to be properly executed.

- Borrower's statement as to source of construction funds.
- Inspecting Architect's Agreement.
- Direct and Indirect Cost Schedules.
- Inspecting Architect's Cost Certification.
- Application and Certification For Payment.
- Architect of Record Certification.
- Engineer of Record Certification.

The following items should be provided to the inspecting architect, enabling him to fulfil his responsibilities.

- Executed Direct Cost Schedule.
- Inspecting Architect's Agreement.
- Inspecting Architect's Cost Certification.
- One complete set of final plans, specifications and soil report.
- All construction contracts and bonds.
- Other agreements respecting work required by the construction documents but not covered by the contracts.
- Copies of all building permits.
- Report from each utility or authority having jurisdiction, respecting date of assured service availability to site; charges for bringing service to site and/or connecting to service; and easements required.
- Current survey, containing certification to ABC the owner and title company showing but not limited to the following:

    Boundaries;

    File reference of appropriate record authority;

    Easements and /or encroachments;

PREPARATION FOR LOAN CLOSING 101

    Restrictions such as building lines, height limitations;

    Natural drainage courses.

- Copy of permanent loan commitment and /or equity purchase agreement.
- Copy of construction loan commitment.
- Contractors project construction schedule.
- List of intended changes or substitutions not reflected in construction documents, budget or schedule costs.
- Addenda to the plans, specifications or other construction documents.
- Any additional information deemed necessary to fulfill responsibilities.

Enclosed for execution at the appropriate time are the following:

- Engineered fill certification.
- Foundation completion certification.

If we can be of any assistance with these items or any other construction loan questions, please do not hesitate to contact us.

EXHIBIT B

ARCHITECT OF RECORD CERTIFICATION   ABC **Number:**

Project Name:

Address:

Date:

TO: ABC CONSTRUCTION LENDING INSTITUTION

I hereby certify that the <u>attached</u> detailed listing of plans and specifications, including all changes and modifications to and including the date hereof, have either been prepared by or under the supervision of the undersigned. Further, said plans and specifications fully comply with all applicable federal, state, municipal and local laws and ordinances, deed restrictions, restrictive convenants and/or other matters of record affecting construction of the improvements as set forth in the title insurance policy issued and are identical with those upon which the building permit is predicated. The said plans and specifications are complete in all respects containing all details necessary for a building which, when built in accordance therewith will be ready for occupancy except as follows:

Our contract with the borrower requires that the undersigned provide the necessary supervision during construction.

_____   Signed:
Borrowers Authorized Signature

Registration Number
and State:

Firm Name:

Address:

Architect's Seal   Phone Number:

EXHIBIT C

TO: INSPECTING ARCHITECT
FROM: ABC CONSTRUCTION LENDING INSTITUTION

A construction loan commitment has been issued for the above-noted project. Your firm has been designated to perform necessary analysis and field inspections.

The scope of your services will include but not be limited to the following:

- Evaluate all contruction related documentation including plans, specifications, soil report, contracts, etc., for obvious errors, omissions and departure from the construction loan documents.

- Based on the above evaluation as background information, review the construction (hard) cost breakdown schedule for adequacy of content, total value and execute our inspecting architect's cost certification.

- Make physicial site inspections, for the purpose of evaluating construction (hard) cost payment requests and provide a certification to ABC that in your opinion there is sufficient time and funds to complete contruction.

- Advise ABC of any discrepencies in the costs or general acceptance of executed work in the form of a short narrative report each month or by phone when conditions dictate.

The borrower will be contacting you shortly to execute our Inspecting Architect's Agreement and provide you with additional information and documents.

Should you have any questions, please do not hesitate to contact us.

EXHIBIT D

INSPECTING ARCHITECT'S AGREEMENT   ABC **Number:**

Project Name:

Address:

Date:

TO: ABC CONSTRUCTION LENDING INSTITUTION

I hereby agree to evaluate, with necessary supporting data provided by the undersigned borrower, the proposed construction (hard) cost breakdown schedule, make physical site inspections and review all application and certificate for payment requests. Each review is to ascertain, with reference to direct costs, that the amount of the request is consistent with the work accomplished and that sufficient time and funds remain to complete the project. A brief narrative report, accompanied with color photographs showing construction status, will be submitted to advise ABC of any construction problems which have developed. In addition, I agree to engage an engineer to perform the necessary work required to executive ABC Foundation Completion Certification.

Under this agreement there will be an initial fee of $_____ to cover all preparations and review of the construction (hard) cost schedule. In addition, a charge of $_____ per inspection and payment request review will be made excluding expenses which we estimate to be $_____ per request. It is estimated that _____ inspections will be required through completion, understood to be not later than _____. For further clarification of costs attached is an hourly fee schedule.

It is acknowledge that I am under _separate_ agreement to perform required inspections for the permanent lender at $_____.

Invoices for services under this agreement are to be submitted after initial cost review and thereafter every month to the borrower. Delinquency in payment of fee is to be brought to the attention of ABC within thirty days and further draw request approval will be withheld unitl compensation is made.

_____   Signed:
Borrower's Authorized Signature

Registration No.
and State:

Firm Name:

Address:

Phone:

EXHIBIT E

ENGINEER OF RECORD CERTIFICATION   ABC **Number:**

Project Name:

Address:

Date:

TO: ABC CONSTRUCTION LENDING INSTITUTION

    I hereby certify that I have analyzed the foundation design of the *attached* listing of plans and specifications, with supporting data (borings, soil reports, etc.) and find that to the best of my knowledge it is adequate to support what is planned and specified.

    The design bearing value of the soil is _____ lbs. per square foot. Where piles are to be used please note type and capacity below.

    I have been engaged by the borrower to provide the necessary supervision during construction.

Conditions or qualifications to the above (if any):

_____

Borrower's Authorized Signature

Signed:

Registration Number
and State:

Firm Name:

Address:

Engineer's Seal   Phone Number:

EXHIBIT F

ENGINEERED FILL CERTIFICATION   ABC **Number:**

Project Name:

Address:

Date:

TO: ABC CONSTRUCTION LENDING INSTITUTION

    We, having been approved as supervising soils engineer for the noted project by ABC CONSTRUCTION, do hereby certify that the engineered fill in place was compacted to at least _____% of maximum laboratory density at optimum moisture content (or _____% relative density) and is capable of safely supporting foundation loads at a bearing capacity of _____ pounds per square foot.

    We further certify that we have: (a) approved the fill material selected, (b) performed all necessary laboratory control tests on the fill material, (c) inspected and approved the stripped subgrade prior to placement of any fill, (d) continuously inspected the placement of fill and performed all necessary field testing, (e) observed that all work related to soil compaction has been done in accordance with the recommendations of the soil report as prepared by _____, and in accordance with plans and specifications accepted by ABC.

    It is our opinion that based upon our calculations, the total settlement of the building foundations placed on this fill will be a maximum of _____ inch(es), with a maximum post-contruction differential settlement between adjacent column footings of _____ inches.

Conditions or qualifications to the above (if any):

Signed:

Registration Number
and State:

Firm Name:

Address:

Engineer's Seal   Phone Number:

EXHIBIT G

FOUNDATION COMPLETION CERTIFICATION

ABC **Number:**

Project Name:

Address:

Date:

TO: ABC CONSTRUCTION LENDING INSTITUTION

    I, having inspected the construction of the foundation at adequate intervals (a total of _____ inspections having been made) and said foundations having been completed, certify that to the best of my knowledge these foundations have been installed in accordance with the plans and specifications accepted by ABC CONSTRUCTION, and are proper and satisfactory in all respects. I further certify that an inspection was made after excavations but prior to pouring of concrete for foundations, and that the minimum bearing value of the soil was at least equal to the design bearing value. Where piles have been used their installation is in a manner that will insure design capacity.

    A Foundation Survey has been provided by the borrower as supporting data and containing a certification to ABC CONSTRUCTION, and the Title Company as follows:

    This is to certify that on this date I made an accurate survey on the ground of the property shown and described hereon, and that this survey locates all lines (including all building setbacks as required by matters of record and the municipality having jurisdiction over the development of such property), dimensions and improvements, easements and/or rights-of-way; that the property has access to dedicated, abutting public streets, as shown hereon; and, that there are no encroachments or protrusions affecting such property.

Conditions or qualifications to the above (if any):

Signed:

Registration Number
and State:

Firm Name:

Address:

Engineer's Seal

Phone:

EXHIBIT H

Page ____ of ____ Pages

ABC CONSTRUCTION LENDING INSTITUTION

APPLICATION FOR PAYMENT **Direct (Hard) Cost** **Period From** ____________ **To** ____________

Item No. (1)	Description of Work (2)	Scheduled Cost (3)	Work Complete: Previous Applications (4)	Work Complete: This Application (5)	Work Complete: Paid by Borrower (6)	Stored Material (Attach Schedule) (7)	Total Completed and Stored to Date 4+5+6+7 (8)	%	Balance to Finish (9)	Retainage (10)	Sub-Contractor (11)
	Base Building Costs:										
	Total or Subtotal										

Note:
- Items shown with asterisk are to be paid in full by Borrower.
- Only gross amounts (and exclusive of cents) are to be shown.
- Amounts shown as stored material are to be transferred to previous applications on next application.

REQUEST NO. ____________

ABC **NO.** ____________

ABC CONSTRUCTION LENDING INSTITUTION

APPLICATION FOR PAYMENT **Direct (Hard) Cost** Period From _____ To _____

Page ___ of ___ Pages

Item No. (1)	Description of Work (2)	Scheduled Cost (3)	Work Complete		Paid by Borrower (6)	Stored Material (Attach Schedule) (7)	Total Completed and Stored to Date 4+5+6+7 (8)	%	Balance to Finish (9)	Retainage (10)	Sub-Contractor (11)
			Previous Applications (4)	This Application (5)							
	Tenant Improvements:										
	Total or Subtotal										

Note:
- Items shown with asterisk are to be paid in full by Borrower
- Only gross amounts (and exclusive of cents) are to be shown
- Amounts shown as stored material are to be transferred to previous applications on next application

REQUEST NO. _____

ABC **NO.** _____

EXHIBIT H (continued)

ABC CONSTRUCTION LENDING INSTITUTION

Page _____ of _____ Pages

APPLICATION FOR PAYMENT **Direct (Hard) Cost Change Orders** Period From _____ To _____

Item No. (1)	Description of Work (2)	Scheduled Cost (3)	Work Complete — Previous Applications (4)	Work Complete — This Application (5)	Paid by Borrower (6)	Stored Material (Attach Schedule) (7)	Total Completed and Stored to Date 4+5+6+7 (8) %	Balance to Finish (9)	Retainage (10)	Sub-Contractor (11)
Total or Subtotal										

Note:
- Items shown with asterisk are to be paid in full by Borrower.
- Only gross amounts (and exclusive of cents) are to be shown.
- Amounts shown as stored material are to be transferred to previous applications on next application.

REQUEST NO. _____

ABC NO. _____

ABC CONSTRUCTION LENDING INSTITUTION

APPLICATION FOR PAYMENT Indirect (Soft) Cost   Period From _____ To _____   Page ___ of ___ Pages

Item No. (1)	Description of Work (2)	Scheduled Cost (3)	Completed to Date		Paid By Borrower (6)	Total Completed 4+5+6 (7) %	Balance to Finish (8)
			Previous Applications (4)	This Application (5)			
	Base Building Costs:						
1.	Land						
2.	Soil Test						
	Inspections						
3.	Surveys						
4.	Architect/Engineer						
	Design						
	Inspection						
5.	Permits						
6.	Closing Costs						
7.	Appraisal Fee						
8.	Legal Fees						
9.	Construction Loan Fees						
10.	Standby Loan Fees						
11.	Title Insurance						
	Total or Subtotal						

Note: • Items shown with asterisk are to be paid in full by Borrower.

REQUEST NO. _____

ABC **NO.** _____

EXHIBIT H (continued)

ABC CONSTRUCTION LENDING INSTITUTION

APPLICATION FOR PAYMENT Indirect (Soft) Cost   Period From _____ To _____   Page ___ of ___ Pages

Item No. (1)	Description of Work (2)	Scheduled Cost (3)	Completed to Date			Total Completed 4+5+6 (7)	Balance to Finish (8)
			Previous Applications (4)	This Application (5)	Paid By Borrower (6)	%	
	Base Building Costs:						
12.	Bonds						
13.	Builders Risk Insurance						
14.	Construction Loan Interest						
15.	Prior Loans						
16.	Taxes						
17.	5% Hard Cost Contingency						
18.	Soft Cost Contingency						
19.	Developers Overhead						
20.	Supervision						
21.	Utility Connections						
22.	Other:						
	Total or Subtotal						

Note:
- Items shown with asterisk are to be paid in full by Borrower.
- Only gross amounts (and exclusive of cents) are to be shown.
- Amounts shown as stored material are to be transferred to previous applications on next application.

REQUEST NO.

ABC NO.

ABC CONSTRUCTION LENDING INSTITUTION

APPLICATION FOR PAYMENT **Indirect (Soft) Cost** **Period From** **To** Page ___ of ___ Pages

Item No. (1)	Description of Work (2)	Scheduled Cost (3)	Completed to Date		Paid By Borrower (6)	Total Completed 4+5+6 (7)	Balance to Finish (8)
			Previous Applications (4)	This Application (5)			
	Tenant and Operating Costs:						
1.	Administration						
2.	Temporary Office						
3.	Tenant Space Planning						
4.	Leasing Fees						
5.	Advertising/Marketing						
6.	Management Fee						
7.	Legal Fees						
8.	Escrow Fees						
9.	Permits						
10.	Audit Fees						
11.	Operating Expenses						
	Total or Subtotal						

Note: • Items shown with asterisk are to be paid in full by Borrower.

REQUEST NO. ___

ABC **NO.** ___

EXHIBIT H (continued)

Page ___ of ___ Pages

ABC CONSTRUCTION LENDING INSTITUTION

APPLICATION FOR PAYMENT Indirect (Soft) Cost Period From ___ To ___

REQUEST NO. ___

ABC NO. ___

Item No. (1)	Description of Work (2)	Scheduled Cost (3)	Completed to Date		Paid By Borrower (6)	Total Completed 4+5+6 (7) %	Balance to Finish (8)
			Previous Applications (4)	This Application (5)			
	Tenant and Operating Costs:						
12.	Insurance						
13.	Utilities						
14.	Elevator Contract						
15.	Cleaning						
16.	Trash Removal						
17.	Maintenance and Repairs						
18.	Landscaping						
19.	Other:						
	Total or Subtotal						

Note: • Items shown with asterisk are to be paid in full by Borrower.

ABC CONSTRUCTION LENDING INSTITUTION

APPLICATION FOR PAYMENT

Indirect (Soft) Cost Changes Orders   Period From _____ To _____

Item No. (1)	Description of Work (2)	Scheduled Cost (3)	Previous Applications (4)	This Application (5)	Paid by Borrower (6)	% (7)	(8)
	Total or Subtotal						

Note:
- Items with asterisk are to be paid in full by the Borrower.

Page ____ of ____ Pages

REQUEST NO. _____
ABC NO. _____

EXHIBIT I

INSPECTING ARCHITECTS
COST CERTIFICATION

ABC **NUMBER**:

Project Name:

Address:

Date:

TO: ABC CONSTRUCTION LENDING INSTITUTION

I, having examined the <u>attached</u> Construction (Direct) Cost Breakdown, certify that in my opinion the cost of $ _____ is sufficient to complete construction in accordance with ABC CONSTRUCTION accepted documents.

This certification is based on supporting data of plans, specifications, soil report, construction contract, loan commitments, etc. which in my opinion provides the necessary information to complete all construction.

Comments (if any):

Signed:

Registration Number
and State:

Firm Name:

Address:

Architect's Seal

Phone Number:

EXHIBIT J

**BORROWER'S STATEMENT AS TO
SOURCE OF CONTRUCTION FUNDS**

ABC **Number:**

Project Name:

Address:

Date:

TO: ABC CONSTRUCTION LENDING INSTITUTION

Construction Costs (Direct & Indirect)	$_____
Land at Cost or Appraised Value	_____
Total Project Cost	$==========
Qualified Permanent Loan Amount (Lowest initial disbursement upon construction completion)	_____
Equity Requirement	$==========

The above Equity Requirement will be satisfied prior to any disbursement of construction loan proceeds, as follows:

- Land, owned free and clear _____
- Actual payment by borrower for budget items shown on Schedule of Values _____
- Escrowed Funds _____
- Letter of Credit _____
- Other collateral (identify) _____

    Total _____

Should the need for additional funds to complete the project become evident during the course of construction, as the result of cost overruns, change orders, reserve deficiencies or other reasons, the required additional funds or collateral will be provided upon request of the Lender, from the following sources:

Mail Address:

_____
Borrower's Authorized Signature

Title:_____

EXHIBIT K

APPLICATION AND CERTIFICATE FOR PAYMENT

ABC No. _____

Period From: _____ To: _____ Request No. _____

Project: _____ Contractor: _____

Borrower: _____ Inspecting Architect: _____

Orig. Direct Costs	_____	Orig. Indirect Cost	_____
Current Cost	_____	**Current Cost**	_____
Completed & Stored	_____	Total Completed	_____
Less Retainage	_____	Less Interest & Fees	_____
Completed to Date	_____	Net Completed to Date	_____

Total Earned to Date (Direct & Indirect)   _____

Less Previous Payments   _____

_____

Less Payments by Borrower   _____

Total Payment Due   _____

CERTIFICATION OF THE CONTRACTOR:
The undersigned hereby certifies:
- that the work herein has been completed in accordance with the plans, specifications and authorized modifications accepted by ABC;
- that all work is in compliance with all laws, ordinances, rules, regulations, and orders of any public authority having jurisdiction; and
- that all items are paid, for which previous certificates were issued and payments received; that the labor and materials for which this advance will pay and which previous advances have paid for, have gone into the construction of the improvements and further, that the property on which the project is being constructed is free and clear of all liens and encumbrances except for liens to be dissolved upon payment of this advance.

Name _____ Company _____

CERTIFICATION OF THE INSPECTING ARCHITECT:
The undersigned hereby certifies:
- that the work herein has been completed generally in accordance with the plans, specifications and authorized modifications accepted by ABC and the contractor is entitled to payment in accordance with the contract and this application for payment.
- that following appropriate completion of foundations, no payment of funds has been authorized without the execution of ABC's Foundation Completion Certification.
- that the sum shown as balance to finish is sufficient in my opinion to complete construction.
- that all stored materials are satisfactorily inventoried and secured.
- as of this date construction is _____ % complete and can be completed by the required date of _____.

Name _____ Firm _____ Lic. # _____ State _____

CERTIFICATION BY THE BORROWER:
The undersigned hereby certifies:
- that all items are paid, for which previous certificates were issued and payments received and that no liens have been filed or other evidence of non-payment received for any obligations included in the Loan Agreement.
- the amount being requested is in order and I hereby approve the request for construction funds in the amount of $ _____.

Name _____ Application Date _____

EXHIBIT L

SAMPLE FORM OF UNCONDITIONAL IRREVOCABLE
LETTER OF CREDIT

BANK LETTERHEAD OR FORM

_____
(Date)

Irrevocable Credit No. _____

TO: ABC CONSTRUCTION LENDING INSTITUTION

Gentlemen:
    We hereby authorize you to value on (X Bank   ) for account of _____ (borrower) for a sum or sums not exceeding a total of _____ ($_____) Dollars available by your draft or drafts at sight. Drafts must be drawn and presented at our office no later than _____, 19____.
    All drafts must be marked "Drawn on (X   Bank) Credit No _____ and all drawings negotiated under this credit must be endorsed on the reverse hereof.
    We hereby agree with the drawers, endorsers and bona fide holders of all drafts drawn on and in compliance with the terms of this credit, that such drafts will be duly honored by presentation to the drawee.
    We specifically waive all our statutory, UCP or other rights, if any, including but not limited to such rights under Article 5, sections 5-112 (1) (a) and (b) of the Uniform Commercial Code, to defer or delay honor or payment of any sight draft.

_____
(Authorized Signature)

7
Title Insurance and Mechanics' Liens

TITLE INSURANCE COVERAGE

Insurance Available

Prior to closing the construction loan, the lender must be assured that it has a first lien on fee simple title to the land (vested in the borrower) and will have such a first lien on the improvements to be constructed. This assurance takes the form of title insurance issued by reputable title insurance company that protects the lender against any loss or damage (not exceeding the amount of insurance) suffered by reason of "any defect in or lien or encumbrance on" the title to the land existing at the effective date of the policy, except for those exceptions to the title insurance specifically set forth in the title insurance policy or known by the insured (lender) and not disclosed to the title insurer. The title insurance may include coverage (or exclusions) relating to: access (or ingress and egress); air rights; covenants, conditions and restrictions; contiguity of several component parcels; easements and rights-of-way; encroachments and projections; inchoate dower and curtesy; leases; leasehold estates and mortgages; liens (e.g., mortgage liens, judgment liens, mechanics' liens, tax liens); lis pendens; navigational servitudes; nonimputation of knowledge from one joint owner to another which has additional insured positions; riparian rights; strips and gores; subsurface rights; successors in interest; surveys; truth-in-lending; usury and zoning. Basically, any type or form of encumbrance (i.e., claim, lien, liability or charge) upon the land may be the subject of title insurance.

Access (or Ingress and Egress). The standard American Land Title Association (ALTA) form of title insurance policy will afford the lender protection against "lack of a right of access to and from the land." (This "right of access" is referred to as a right to "ingress and egress" in The New York Board of Title Underwriters (NYBTU) standard form of policy.) However, when this "right of access" includes the right to enter and leave over the lands of another (sometimes called "right of egress"), affirmative title insurance specifying this right is often sought, particularly when the right of access is material to the project and increases its value. Rights of access typically are in the form of easements and rights-of-way, the descriptions of which should preferably be included within the insured legal description contained in the policy and reflected on the insured survey (hereinafter discussed).

Air Rights. Traditionally, under the common law the ownership of land was considered to extend from the center of the earth to the heavens above. Today, while that concept is still valid, it is not uncommon to find air rights and subsurface rights separated from the surface ownership. Any such division of ownership will be reflected in the title policy. The ownership of or easements affecting the space above the physical surface of the land (that is, air rights) are becoming more and more important and any limitation on the surface ownership will appear in the title policy as an exception. Thus, for example, land in the vicinity of an airport may be subject to navigational easements; inner city land may be subject to light and air easements in favor of adjoining property or that land's developmental rights may have been sold. Under any such circumstances, the lender must assure itself that the proposed building will not intrude into the air rights of others. On the other hand, when the lender's security benefits from air rights over adjoining parcels, so as to enhance the view of those occupying the security or to increase the size and/or height of the proposed project, the existence of these rights should be specified, legally described and insured in the title insurance policy.

Covenants, Conditions and Restrictions. This is a common group of words used to designate the limitations on use to which land may be subject, often providing penalties in the enacting document for failure to comply with stated provisions. These covenants, conditions and restrictions often appear as provisos in deeds and are commonly used by land subdividers on newly platted areas or may be imposed by local ordinances. If any covenants, conditions and restrictions appear in the title report as exceptions to title, the lender must first satisfy itself that the proposed construction is in conformity with the permitted uses for the land; that is, does not violate the covenants, conditions and restrictions. The lender should then require affirmative title insurance asserting that there are no present violations of the covenants, conditions or restrictions and that any future violation will not result in a right of reentry nor forfeiture or reversion of title or in any impairment or loss of the lender's lien.

Contiguity. When the insured land consists of one or more adjoining parcels or adjoins another parcel of land as part of a phased development, it is not uncommon to require title insurance that the adjoining parcels are contiguous. Assuming the facts (as disclosed by the survey) confirm the contiguity of the parcels, the insurance should be readily provided and related to the survey to show the relationship of the parcels.

Easements and Rights-of-Way. The insured property is sometimes benefited by easements and rights-of-way over the lands of others (see discussion of access above). However, at times others will have the "right-of-way" to cross the insured parcel or some other form of easement entitling its holder to a limited use of the land (e.g., laying a sewer, putting up electric power lines). In the latter instance, the lender should require that any such easements and rights-of-way be reflected on the survey and that the title policy insure the accuracy of the survey. In addition, the lender must be assured that the location of these exceptions to title will not interfere with the location and construction of the proposed improvements. In the former instance, the easements should be included in the insured land.

Encroachments and Projections. In situations where walls, fences and hedges, for example, situated on the lender's security, intrude onto the lands of another, the lender should look to the title insurer for protection against any monetary loss occasioned by the enforced removal of these encroachments and projections. This type of insurance is more prevalent in rehabilitation projects (where there is a much greater likelihood of encroachments and projections existing) as opposed to new construction, where for the most part, vacant land is involved or the existing structures are to be torn down and the land cleared before the new construction begins.

If there are any encroachments and projections from the adjoining land onto the lender's security (retractive encroachments), these will most likely be listed as exceptions to the title which the lender should require to be clearly measured on the survey and investigate to determine whether they are material.

Inchoate Dower and Curtesy. In certain states the law grants to a wife (inchoate dower) and/or to a husband (inchoate curtesy), an interest in the lands of the other which ripens into possession and use upon the death of the other. If individual borrowers are involved, these rights may give the construction lender cause for concern. Should these rights appear in the title report as exceptions to the title, the lender should insist that they be cleared either by having the rights waived (if permitted by local law); by having the spouse join in signing the loan documents; or, if the missing spouse's signature is no longer available, by instituting the proper legal and equitable procedures.

Leases. When the property is "preleased"; that is, tenant space leases are entered into prior to construction in anticipation of the premises being completed by a certain date, a priority question may arise if the tenant leases are executed before the construction mortgage is recorded. In such situations, the leases will be listed as exceptions to title unless the lease terms expressly call for subordination to the construction mortgage (typically the language in the lease will read "this lease is subordinate to any and all (first) mortgages or deeds of trust that are or may become liens upon the land") or a separate subordination agreement is entered into between the tenant and the lender. If the leases are so subordinated, they should be listed in a separate schedule to the title insurance policy as a subordinate lien to the lien of the insured mortgage.

Leasehold Estates and Mortgages. When the security for the construction loan consists of a mortgage on the borrower's leasehold estate as opposed to fee title, the lender should require that the title insurance policy insure with respect to the ground lease (that has been recorded) that: (1) the borrower has good and marketable title in and to the ground lease; (2) the borrower has the right to and has assigned the ground lease to the lender; (3) the ground lease is in full force and effect without default or modification other than a modification specifically referred to in the policy; and (4) the lender, as assignee of the ground lessee, has succeeded to all of the estate of the ground lessee in the leasehold estate created by the ground lease as collateral.

Liens. Any encumbrance or charge allowed a creditor upon the lands of a debtor is considered a lien. These may take various forms, the most common of which are mortgage liens, judgment liens, mechanics' liens and tax liens. Claims which ripen or are likely to ripen into liens with the passage of time should be considered here as liens.

If there is a land loan on the property (or a standing loan in the event of a rehab of existing space), the mortgages securing these loans will appear in the title report as liens against the property. To insure the priority of the construction lender's lien, these mortgages must either be released or satisfied of record, or subordinated to the construction loan, including future advances thereunder if any and any renewals, etc. In this latter case, the construction lender should insist upon the final policy expressly stating that each such existing mortgage is subordinate to the lender's insured mortgage and (where applicable) that such subordinate mortgage is also junior to any and all leases that have been or may hereafter be entered into with regard to the property.

Judgment liens reflected in the title report must either be paid in full and satisfied of record or the title company must be persuaded to insure over the lien, obtaining cash or liability (e.g., a bond) satisfactory to it to cover the amount of the lien.

The specific form of mechanic's lien coverage available will, to a large extent, depend upon the priority of the construction mortgage vis-à-vis the mechanic's lien (see page 131). However, in most jurisdictions, the construction lender should require, as a minimum (unless precluded by law), the protection afforded by the most widely used form of standard loan policy, ALTA Loan Policy—1970 (Rev. October 17, 1970), which insures against "Any statutory lien for labor or material which now has gained or hereafter may gain priority over the lien of the insured mortgage, except any such lien arising from an improvement on the land contracted for and commenced subsequent to Date of Policy not financed in whole or in part by proceeds of the indebtedness secured by the insured mortgage which at Date of Policy the insured has advanced or is obligated to advance." The only qualification to this coverage, which may be acceptable to the construction lender, is a pending disbursements clause which often reads as follows:

"Pending disbursement of the full proceeds of the loan secured by the mortgage insured, the Policy only insures the amount actually disbursed, but increases as proceeds are disbursed in good faith and without knowledge of any intervening lien or interest, to or for the account of the mortgagor pursuant to a legal obligation to disburse up to the amount of the Policy. Prior to each disbursement of loan proceeds, title must be continued and intervening liens disposed of, to the satisfaction of the Company."

Tax liens are similar to judgment liens in their treatment except that they must be paid in full rather than "bonded off."

Lis Pendens. In certain jurisdictions, a lis pendens or notice recorded in the public land records indicating that a suit is pending affecting the lands where the notice is recorded, will afford any subsequent judgment arising out of the suit priority over a (construction) mortgage recorded subsequent to the recording of the notice. The approach often taken by lenders when confronted with such a situation is to require that the title insurer "insure over" the lis pendens. Title companies may provide this coverage upon receipt of an indemnity from the borrower and/or a bond in the full amount of the potential judgment. Alternately, the lis pendens can be removed from the land records by posting such a bond with the court where the litigation is taking place.

Navigational Servitudes. When the lender's security is built on land reclaimed from adjacent bodies of navigable water or adjoins navigable waters (those waters which afford a channel for usable commerce), the lender may be confronted with the public's right of navigation over these waters. These rights, commonly referred to as "navigational servitudes," could result in the enforced removal of fill along the banks of the waters and/or of any improvements erected on such reclaimed land or fill. Title insurance coverage can be helpful here by insuring the lender against any loss or damage by reason of any such enforced removal without due compensation; or, if such compensation is not obtainable, by assisting the parties in locating the improvements over such part of the land not subject to possible enforced removal.

Nonimputation. Since title insurance coverage will exclude title defects known to the lender and not disclosed to the title insurer, problems could arise in a situation where one or more joint owners has knowledge of a title defect not known nor disclosed to the insured joint owner who is also mortgagee. Due to the relationship of the participants, the knowledge of one may be imputed as being the knowledge of all. To resolve this dilemma and safeguard the position of each participant, a "nonimputation" endorsement to the mortgagee's title insurance policy should be sought wherein the definition of "known to the insured" is restricted to actual knowledge and not knowledge imputed to the mortgagee as such by reason of joint ownership.

Riparian Rights. Riparian rights are defined by Blacks' Law Dictionary as being "the rights of the owners of lands on the banks of watercourses, relating to the water, its use, ownership of soil under the stream, accretions, etc." The watercourses may include lakes, rivers, streams or brooks and whether the watercourses are navigable or not is a question of fact. However, if a watercourse is self-contained within the insured land, no ostensible title problems arise. If the watercourse is not self-contained; that is, it flows through the land of others, title problems do arise for the borrower cannot interfere with the riparian rights of such other land owners; that is, the borrower cannot interfere with the natural flow of water onto the lands of others. This restriction on use of the watercourse and the lands thereunder will appear as an exception in the title insurance policy and may be material to the construction lender, depending upon the proximity of the proposed improvements to the watercourse and/or whether any changes in the watercourse or underlying land are contemplated as part of the new development.

Strips and Gores.   If any strips and gores are disclosed in the title report, a certification of their ownership must be made. If ownership is unkown or is vested in a party other than the borrower, the title company should be persuaded to insure over it. If this is not possible, the lender must determine whether the strip or gore is material to its security and if so it may be necessary for the borrower to acquire little to the strip or gore in order for the construction loan to close.

Subsurface Rights.   When a party other than the borrower has the right to ownership of things beneath the physical surface of the property, the lender faces possible loss as a result of damage to the surface occasioned by the exercise of these subsurface rights. Often, protection against surface damage to the land is contractually and/or legally provided for in the mineral and oil and gas reservations themselves and/or in certain states by statute. When this is not the case, the title insurer should be asked to afford protection against any such loss. If this is not possible, the lender must gauge the likelihood of subsurface activity taking place and then make a business decision whether the risk is acceptable. The extent of the subsurface rights still owned by the borrower will be a factor in the lender's decision process. An additional problem relates to the difficulty in defining exactly what constitutes "surface" and/or "subsurface" area.

Successors in Interest.   If the construction loan documents are intended to be assigned to a permanent lender upon completion of construction, the construction lender would be wise to conform its documentations to the long-term lender's requirements and to have the title insurer agree in advance to an assignment of the policy to the permanent lender. This, of course, cannot substitute for a clean policy at the time of closing the permanent loan, for the permanent lender will assuredly insist upon the effective date of the policy being extended to the date of the assignment to it of the loan documents, but it may serve to facilitate such closing by insuring the availability of a permanent loan policy with a title insurer familiar with the title to the land.

Surveys. Survey coverage afforded by title insurance companies insures against title defects arising from a consideration of the relationship between the physical improvements upon the insured land and the record title. In order for this coverage to be available, the title insurer must be furnished a current survey of the property satisfactory to it. If not, the policy will contain a standard exception reading, "any state of facts an accurate survey would show." When a satisfactory survey is available but is not current, the exception would read, "any state of facts an accurate survey (after the date of the last acceptable survey) would show." Survey coverage obviously grows in importance as construction progresses and improvements are placed upon the insured land. However, it is relevant even when raw land is concerned by locating existing or record easements which can be plotted against the proposed location of the improvements and by disclosing any encroachments and projections by improvements onto the insured land from adjoining property.

Truth in Lending. The standard title insurance loan policy excludes from its coverage loss based upon any consumer credit protection or truth-in-lending law. This exclusion is not generally material in commercial real estate financing; however, if a lender has any doubt that the transaction is exempted or excepted from the Truth-in-Lending Act, it can seek an endorsement to the title insurance policy which will insure it against loss or damage resulting from a valid exercise of the right of rescission conferred by the Act.

Usury. Usury is treated similar to truth in lending as an area not insured against as part of the title insurer's standard loan policy. However, there the similarity ends, for usury considerations are material in commercial real estate financing (although less so now than in previous years as more and more states raise their usury ceilings). To safeguard against possible usury violations an endorsement to the title insurance policy should be sought which typically will insure against loss or damage that the lender may sustain by reason of the entry of any court order of judgment which constitutes a final determination and adjudges the lien of the insured mortgage invalid or unenforceable as to principal and/or interest due on the note secured thereby on the ground that the loan evidenced by said note is usurious; and/or calls for the repayment of any part of the principal and interest paid to the lender or the payment of a penalty by lender on the ground that the amount of interest so paid violated the usury laws. (Note: This form of endorsement is not available in all states and will in all instances be conditioned upon the interest due and/or paid having been computed in accordance with the provisions of the note and mortgage.)

Zoning. Zoning and other governmental limitations also are excluded ordinarily in the general exceptions from title insurance coverage. Hence, lenders concerned with possible zoning violations will once again be seeking protection by way of an endorsement to the standard loan policy. Such endorsements relating to zoning in those jurisdictions where available at all, will typically describe the classification in which the property is zoned and the use or uses permitted under such classification. They will *not* insure that the actual (or intended) use of the property complies with the permitted uses for the property.

Amount of Insurance

The amount of title insurance is a material consideration since it sets the upper limit of the loss or damage that the title insurer is responsible for. Generally, this amount will never exceed the full face amount of the construction loan and at any one time will not exceed the amount of funds advanced by the lender to date. This limitation of coverage of funds advanced to date is typically contained (as limited by the printed conditions in the title insurance policy which bar negligence actions and delete consequential damages) in the pending disbursements clause, a sample of which is contained in the discussion of mechanic's liens (see page 125).

Title Insurance Policies

In 1975, the title insurance industry came out with a new construction loan policy form which offered less protection to lenders than they had previously been accustomed to. The main difference between the (then) new construction loan policy and the 1970 ALTA lenders' policy related to the mechanic's lien coverage. The title insurance industry argued that the furnishing of mechanic's lien coverage during construction went beyond the tenets of title insurance coverage and had been assumed without a commensurate increase in premium. The title insurance industry had suffered (and still does suffer) substantial losses due to mechanic's lien claims and objected to the language in the ALTA loan policy which afforded protection against any statutory liens for labor or material which "... *hereafter may gain priority*" over the lien of the insured mortgage. The new construction loan policy proffered by the title insurance industry hit the lending community like a "bombshell" and in essence was rejected as an acceptable form of policy. Hence, most construction lenders still insist upon obtaining the 1970 ALTA form with the mechanic's lien coverage afforded thereby or by virtue of special endorsements to the title policy.

There are a few states (most notably, Texas) where by statute, the ALTA form is not available and title insurance companies are prohibited from issuing mechanic's lien or other coverage. This does not seem to have had a material impact upon real estate investment in these states. Lenders seem to have adjusted their underwriting practices and loan administration procedures adequately to assure themselves internally that the title insurance coverage that is available elsewhere will not be necessary here. The lack of coverage is simply an additional risk of doing business, which so far has been found to be an acceptable one.

Title Insurance Companies

Most title insurance policies are written by companies that are members of the ALTA. Typically, the initial title insurer is selected by the borrower with the lender retaining the right to approve the borrower's choice. This approval is usually readily forthcoming except in instances where the lender has had past unfavorable dealings with the title insurer or the lender requires special coverage that the chosen title insurer is unwilling to provide but that is available from competing companies. A third reason for rejecting a proffered title insurance company relates to the financial net worth of the company. If the title insurer is undercapitalized or the lender feels that the liquid assets of the title insurer are not sufficient to meet possible claims, the lender must require reinsurance from another title company or companies.

The most widely used form of reinsurance is the 1961 ALTA Facultative Reinsurance Agreement. However, lenders should insist that this form be supplemented with a direct access agreement with the reinsurer. The most desirable form is joint and several coverage.

THE CONSTRUCTION MORTGAGE VERSUS THE MECHANIC'S LIEN—A QUESTION OF PRIORITY

Nature and Scope of Mechanics' Liens

The mechanic's lien is defined by Black's Law Dictionary as being "a claim created by law for the purpose of securing priority of payment of the price or value of work performed and materials furnished in erecting or repairing a building or other structure, and as such attaches to the land as well as buildings and improvements erected thereon." This priority afforded the mechanic's lienor places the mechanic's lien claimant in direct conflict with the construction lender who is looking for a first or priority lien against the property.

To determine which party has priority, it will be of benefit to have a better understanding of the nature and scope of the mechanic's lien claim. Since the mechanic's lien is "a claim created by law," in order for it to be sustained, there must first be specific enabling legislation permitting such a claim. In this regard, since Maryland enacted the first mechanic's lien law in the United States in 1796, followed by Pennsylvania in 1803, every state in the nation and the District of Columbia have either enacted mechanic's lien laws and/or mandated or conferred mechanics' liens by constitution (e.g., California Const. Art: XX, Sect. 15 and Texas Const. Art. XVI, Sect. 37). The question then is not whether enabling legislation exists, but rather whether the party asserting the claim and the claim itself fall within the purview of such legislation. Unfortunately, the application and operation of the various enabling legislation differ from jurisdiction to jurisdiction and attempts to enact a uniform mechanic's lien law (despite repeated attempts by the title insurance industry) have so far been unsuccessful.

Two Types of Legislation

Despite the varied application and operation of the different mechanic's lien statutes, most enabling legislation, including provisions relating to the amount of claim that may be asserted and the parties permitted to assert such claims, can be categorized into one of two types.

The "New York" System. The more restrictive type of legislation is commonly referred to as the "New York" system. Statutes following the New York rule generally limit the liability of an owner (and consequently, the amount of lien that may possibly come ahead of the construction mortgage) to the amount then due and payable under the construction contract at the time a claimant files a notice of lien, plus any amount which may become due under the contract thereafter. In other words, the potential liability at any time a notice of mechanic's lien is filed is limited to the actual construction contract price less any payments made to the general contractor pursuant to the contract. The rights of the subcontractors and suppliers are derivative, and if the general contractor has been paid in full or even if the particular party that retained their services has been paid in full pursuant to the contract, they have no right to file a lien against the property.

Although the states following the New York system severely limit the amount of claim that may be asserted by a mechanic's lienor, they are quite liberal in whom they permit to file mechanics' liens, extending such right to lower-tier subcontractors and suppliers. This expansiveness is somewhat misleading, however, since if the party next in line in the chain of work has been paid, the lower-tier subcontractors and suppliers will not have a lienable claim.

The following states are believed to follow the New York system:

Alabama	New Hampshire
Connecticut	New Jersey
District of Columbia	New York
Florida	North Carolina
Illinois	South Carolina
Louisiana	South Dakota
Massachusetts	Texas
Mississippi	Utah
Nevada	Vermont
	Virginia

The "Pennsylvania" System. The second type of mechanic's lien legislation is commonly referred to as the "Pennsylvania" system. States following the Pennsylvania rule generally provide for the full value of all claims to be lienable regardless of the amount due or paid the general contractor. Thus, payments made to the general contractor prior to the filing of a notice of mechanic's lien by a subcontractor or materialman will not serve to limit or restrict the amount of the mechanic's lien claim. However, since the potential liability for mechanics' liens is quite broad as opposed to the restrictive nature of the New York system, the right to file a mechanic's lien is generally limited only to first-tier contractors and suppliers.

The following states are believed to follow the Pennsylvania system:

Alaska	Minnesota
Arizona	Missouri
Arkansas	Montana
California	Nebraska
Colorado	New Mexico
Delaware	North Dakota
Georgia	Ohio
Hawaii	Oklahoma
Idaho	Oregon
Indiana	Pennsylvania
Iowa	Rhode Island
Kansas	Tennessee
Kentucky	Washington
Maine	West Virginia
Maryland	Wisconsin
Michigan	Wyoming

Summary. Mechanic's lien rights under the New York system are "derivative," with such rights being extended to lower-tier subcontractors and suppliers, but with recovery limited to the amount owing by the owner to the general contractor (i.e., the actual general contract price less any payments already made pursuant to the contract). Mechanic's lien rights under the Pennsylvania system are "direct," with such rights being limited to first-tier contractors and suppliers, but with no limit on the amount of legitimate claim that may be recovered.

Legislative Requirements

Since a mechanic's lien claim is a creature of statute, in order to sustain a claim, the requirements of the particular enabling legislation must be strictly complied with. Apart from being a "permitted" lienor and filing for the proper amount of lienable claim as previously mentioned, the claim must be for "work performed and materials furnished in erecting or repairing a building." Generally, and by way of example, this would include the value of steel supplied to the site and the cost of implacing the steel in the building; but would not include the cost of fuel to run the building nor premiums paid for workman's compensation or public liability insurance. This distinction is true regardless of whether the legislation follows the New York or the Pennsylvania systems.

The distinction between the two types of mechanic's lien legislation becomes apparent once again when the more technical requirements of the legislation are investigated; for example, provisions governing the time for filing, contents of claim, notice and service of notice. Using the two lead states as examples, under the New York statute, a mechanic's lien claim may be filed at any time during the progress of the work or the furnishing of materials up to four months after the last item of work or materials is furnished for the project. Under the Pennsylvania statute, a mechanic's lien must be filed within four months after completion of the actual claimants work. It is clear that this distinction has as its origin the difference in the amount of lienable claim permitted.

Priority of Lien

Assuming the mechanic's lien claim has been properly filed by a protected party for the alloted amount and seeking recovery for covered good and services, one of the more important issues to be determined is when the filed lien will become effective (i.e., when it attaches to the land and improvements). To a large extent this will determine the priority of the mechanic's lien claim vis-à-vis the construction mortgage. Unfortunately, there is no common rule controlling the effective date which can be either the date of the construction contract, the date work has commenced on the project, the date of filing or the date the claimant either commenced or completed his work.

Generally, the priority of the mechanic's lienor will be lower than that of the construction mortgagee unless his lien attached before the recording of the mortgage. However, in a few jurisdictions the mechanic's lien claim has an absolute priority regardless of when the lien attached; and in certain other jurisdictions the construction mortgage will have priority over a previously effective mechanic's lien claim.

Priority to Mechanic's Lienor. Where the priority is given to subcontractors and materialmen over the construction mortgage regardless of the date the mechanic's lien attaches to the land (e.g., Illinois), a prudent construction lender should insist upon title insurance protection against mechanics' liens at the time the construction loan closes and at the time of each loan disbursement. However, due to the priority nature of the mechanic's lien claim, the insurance provided by the title insurer will be limited to protection against liens arising from work for which payment has been made with funds actually being disbursed by the title insurer (or by the lender with the title insurer's approval). In these jurisdictions, it would be advisable for construction lenders to require advances to be placed in a construction loan escrow controlled by the title company. The title insurer will usually insist on lien waivers and/or paid receipts from the subcontractors and materialmen prior to disbursing any funds from the escrow account. It will also require the borrower to execute some form of indemnity agreement holding the title insurer harmless should it suffer any losses to the lender as a result of the afforded mechanic's lien coverage.

Priority to Construction Lender. Where the construction mortgage has an absolute priority over mechanic's lienors, the lender must be sure to comply with the conditions imposed by law to create such superior lien. Generally, as in New York State, these conditions will consist of filing the building loan agreement in the County Clerk's Office where the property is located before recording the construction mortgage and inserting a trust fund clause in the agreement which calls for the funds advanced to the borrower to be held in trust to be used to pay for the cost of improvements before they can be used for other purposes.

This absolute priority will apply to all funds advanced pursuant to the terms of the building loan agreement until such time as a mechanic's lien is filed. The lender will be offered no protection if it continues to advance funds after such a lien has been filed. To protect itself, the lender should insist on receiving an updated title report (and endorsement extending the effective date of the title insurance policy) at the time of each advance to verify that no liens have been placed on the property since the time of the last advance.

The priority afforded the construction mortgage may also be lost if the building loan agreement is modified, if the lender permits the parties to deviate from the terms of the agreement (e.g., it waives the architect's inspection) without the consent of all adverse parties and/or should the lender participate with the borrower in a diversion of the trust funds (e.g., it permits advanced funds to be used for the payment of a tax lien rather than for construction).

In states where the lender's construction mortgage has priority over mechanics' liens, the lender may occasionally advance funds directly to the borrower without awaiting a title report. However, this procedure bears certain risks and should be undertaken only if the borrower and general contractor have a proven track record and a sound financial base. In addition, if the lender agrees to do this for one advance, it should insist that prior to the next advance the borrower submit the paid receipts and lien waivers or releases along with a title report that evidences that as of the last advance, the subcontractors and materialmen were actually paid, and that no liens were filed. In other words, an exposure of this sort should be limited to a single advance and then only if such advance is not disproportionately large in relation to the total loan or other advances.

Title Insurance

In some instances, lenders may require initial title insurance protection against mechanics' liens for the full amount of the construction loan, notwithstanding the fact that all of the loan proceeds have not as yet been disbursed. Such protection is not always available, is very costly and the insurer will almost always require that it control the disbursement of the loan proceeds. These latter two points can be the cause of major contention between the borrower and lender. In any event, regardless of whether full or partial mechanic's lien coverage is obtained from the title insurer, no form of coverage will protect the lender against liens arising from improvements contracted for subsequent to the effective date of the title policy, liens not financed by the proceeds of the particular construction loan, or liens arising from work that the lender is obligated to finance after the date of the policy.

Precautionary Measures

Despite the availability of title insurance protection against mechanics' liens, the lender should still take precautionary measures in order to preserve the priority of its mortgage. For example, if the effective date of the mechanic's lien relates back to the date work commenced on the project (e.g., as in Texas), the construction lender would be well advised to record its mortgage (and in certain states advance a portion of the loan proceeds as well) prior to any ground breaking. The situation is more problematical when the attachment date is tied to the execution of the construction contract. Lenders are understandably reluctant to advance any funds unless they have a firm handle on the projected costs of the project. This is not possible until a firm fixed price construction contract is executed.

Bonding

In addition to title insurance coverage, lenders have sought protection against the filing of mechanic's lien claims through the use of bonding, with the lender named as dual obligee on the bonds. Generally, bonds are furnished by the general contractor as principal and either guarantee that the construction contract will be performed in accordance with its provisions (the performance bond) or guarantee that all labor and materials will be paid (the payment bond). When the owner is also the developer/general contractor and is thus not "bondable," lenders will often require that the major subcontractors be bonded instead. In the past, bonding has been required mainly on public works projects, but in today's high interest environment, it is being increasingly required on private projects as well.

State Survey

The survey appended to this chapter breaks down, on a state-by-state basis, answers to the following questions:

1. Can a mortgage priority obtain priority over subsequently filed mechanic's liens, and if so, how?
2. Are obligatory advances required to obtain priority?
3. Will filed liens take priority over subsequent advances (i.e., regardless of its obligatory nature, will an advance made after the filing of a mechanic's lien be inferior to such lien)?

The answers were furnished to the author by Lawyers Title Insurance Company of Richmond Virginia, one of the major title insurance companies. Lawyers Title did the research necessary to provide this information in order to enable it to formulate the form and type of protection against mechanics' liens that it would be able to offer in the various states.

Caveat. Since mechanic's lien statutes are subject to legislative whim and judicial interpretation, the answers set forth on the chart may not be 100% correct. The information is furnished for use as a convenient guide and *under no circumstances* should the answers set forth be taken as definitive with regard to any particular question of priority.

Conclusion

Although the heading of this section describes the relationship between the construction lender and the mechanic's lienor in terms of "a question of priority," and lenders undoubtedly go to great lengths to safeguard the priority of their mortgage against mechanic's liens, priority alone does not afford the lender the protection it needs. This is true notwithstanding the availability of title insurance and bonding. What the lender requires is that the project be completed on a timely basis and its construction loan repaid. This may not happen if the project is continually beset with labor unrest and completion of construction is delayed due to disputes over payment to contractors and suppliers. Priority of the construction mortgage will insure successful litigation and title coverage and bonds may insure that an outside source of funds will be available to pay off the mechanic's lien claims should they prevail. *But,* they will not prevent the cessation of work by disgruntled contractors nor guarantee that a court will permit construction to proceed while the mechanic's lien claim is being litigated.

In the interim, construction costs may rise above acceptable limits (with the lender's interest reserve depleted) and the viability of the permanent loan or equity purchase commitment may be jeopardized (a catastrophe in most instances).

The bottom line is that regardless of the priority in existence or protection available, there can never be a substitute for good loan underwriting or for proper loan administration whereby the lender closely monitors the progress of construction and assures itself that the loan proceeds are actually going into the project.

STATE	CAN A MORTGAGE PRIORITY OBTAIN PRIORITY OVER SUBSEQUENTLY FILED MECHANICS' LIENS, AND, IF SO, HOW?	ARE OBLIGATORY ADVANCES REQUIRED TO OBTAIN PRIORITY?	WILL FILED LIENS TAKE PRIORITY OVER SUBSEQUENT ADVANCES (I.E., REGARDLESS OF ITS OBLIGATORY NATURE, WILL AN ADVANCE MADE AFTER THE FILING OF A MECHANICS' LIEN BE INFERIOR TO SUCH LIEN)?
Alabama	No priority can be obtained		
Arizona	Yes. Priority can be obtained by recording mortgage prior to any visible commencement of work or furnishing of materials.	Yes	No
Arkansas	Yes. Mortgages must be recorded prior to commencement of building or improvement.	Yes	Not if mortgage makes specific provisions for the future advances and if they are obligatory.
California	Yes. Priority can be obtained by recording mortgage prior to any visible commencement of work or furnishing of materials.	Yes	No
Colorado	Recordation prior to commencement of work. However, this cannot be relied on because the statute provides for a lien for persons preparing plats, plans, drawings and so forth. Therefore, date of commencement cannot be determined.		
Connecticut	Priority obtained by prior recordation and in compliance with 49-3 of the Connecticut Code. If any work is commenced prior to the recording of the mortgage, it is necessary to obtain waivers from all laborers and suppliers and the mortgagee must be in compliance with 49-3.	Yes	Yes, if in accordance with 49-3.

Delaware	Yes, by recordation of the mortgage or deed of trust prior to the commencement of construction. Code section 25-2118 and 25-2718.	No. Code Section 25-2118.	No, not if the mortgage or deed of trust was recorded prior to the commencement of construction and the advances are made within 5 years of the date of such mortgage or deed of trust. Code Section 25-2118 and 25-2718.
District of Columbia	Yes, but only as to advances made before the filing of notice of a M&M lien. Code Section 38-109.	Not applicable. Priority cannot be obtained for advances made after the filing of a M&M lien, even if such advances are obligatory. Code Section 38-109.	Yes. Code Section 38-109.
Florida	Priority can be obtained by filing for record of mortgage prior to filing for record of notice of commencement. Recordation prior to commencement of work.	No	No
Georgia		Yes, to continue priority.	Only if advances are optional.
Hawaii	Priority can be obtained by filing for record of mortgage prior to the time of the visible commencement of operation. Also, where a mortgage is recorded prior to the date of completion, and all or a portion of the money advanced under and secured by the mortgage is thereafter used for the purpose of paying for the improvement, the mortgage shall be entitled to the extent of the payments, to priority over liens of mechanics and materialmen, but no such priority shall be allowed unless the mortgage recites that the purpose of the mortgage is to secure the monies advanced	No Hawaii statuatory authority on this.	No Hawaii statuatory authority on this.

141

(*continued*)

STATE	CAN A MORTGAGE PRIORITY OBTAIN PRIORITY OVER SUBSEQUENTLY FILED MECHANICS' LIENS, AND, IF SO, HOW?	ARE OBLIGATORY ADVANCES REQUIRED TO OBTAIN PRIORITY?	WILL FILED LIENS TAKE PRIORITY OVER SUBSEQUENT ADVANCES (I.E., REGARDLESS OF ITS OBLIGATORY NATURE, WILL AN ADVANCE MADE AFTER THE FILING OF A MECHANICS' LIEN BE INFERIOR TO SUCH LIEN)?
	for the purpose of paying for the improvement in whole or in part. Payments made in good faith to the general contractor for such purposes shall be presumed to have been used for the purpose of paying for the improvements.		
Idaho	Recordation prior to commencement of work.	Yes	No
Illinois	No priority can be obtained.		
Indiana	No priority can be obtained.		
Iowa	Yes. Priority may be obtained by recording a mortgage prior to any visible commencement of work or furnishing of materials.	Yes	No
Kansas	Yes. Priority may be obtained by recording a mortgage prior to any visible commencement of work or furnishing of materials.	Yes	No
Kentucky	Priority obtained as to each advance on recorded mortgage if at date of such advance no lien has been filed for record and mortgagee has received no notice of claim of lien.		
Louisiana	Priority can be obtained by recordation of the mortgage and deliv-	No	No

State		
	ery of the note secured thereby to the lender prior to the commencement of work or delivery of materials to the premises *and prior* to the recordation of the building contract.	
Maine	No priority can be obtained.	
Maryland	Yes, by recordation of the mortgage or deed of trust prior to the commencement of the building. *Real Property* section 9-107(b).	No, not if the mortgage or deed of trust was recorded prior to the commencement of the building. *Real Property* section 9-107(b).
Mass.	Priority based on recordation of mortgage prior to commencement of any work and prior to notice of contract.	Yes
Michigan	No priority can be obtained.	
Minnesota	Recordation prior to commencement of work.	Priority continues as to obligatory advances.
Mississippi	Recordation prior to commencement of work but extends only until notice of lien is filed. This priority extends only to the extent that the money was used in the construction.	Priority may be lost by optional advances.
Missouri	No priority can be obtained.	
Montana	No priority can be obtained.	
Nebraska	Yes. Mortgage must be recorded prior to commencement of construction.	Not if subsequent advances are obligatory under the prerecorded mortgage.
Nevada	Recordation prior to commencement of work.	Will take priority over optional advances.
New Hampshire	Priority based on prior recordation of mortgage and disbursements in accordance with statute (447:12a).	Seemingly yes, if in accordance with the statute.

143

(*continued*)

STATE	CAN A MORTGAGE PRIORITY OBTAIN PRIORITY OVER SUBSEQUENTLY FILED MECHANICS' LIENS, AND, IF SO, HOW?	ARE OBLIGATORY ADVANCES REQUIRED TO OBTAIN PRIORITY?	WILL FILED LIENS TAKE PRIORITY OVER SUBSEQUENT ADVANCES (I.E., REGARDLESS OF ITS OBLIGATORY NATURE, WILL AN ADVANCE MADE AFTER THE FILING OF A MECHANICS' LIEN BE INFERIOR TO SUCH LIEN)?
New Jersey	Yes, but only as to advances made before the filing of an M & M lien. Code section 2 A:44-88.	Not applicable. Priority cannot be obtained for advances made after the filing of an M&M lien, even if such advances are obligatory. Code section 2 A:44-88.	Yes. Code section 2 A:44-88.
New Mexico	Yes. Priority may be obtained by recording a mortgage prior to any visible commencement of work or furnishing of materials.	Yes	No
New York	Yes, if mortgage contains lien clause and building or loan agreement recorded.	No	No
North Carolina	Yes. Priority may be obtained by recording a mortgage prior to any visible commencement of work or furnishing of materials.	Yes	No
North Dakota	Yes. Mortgage must be recorded prior to time of actual and visible beginning of improvement on the ground *except* no permits for construction loan applying to "complete and independent building."	Yes	Probably yes.
Ohio	Recordation prior to commencement of work.	Yes	Will take priority over optional advances.

Oklahoma	Yes. Priority may be obtained by recording a mortgage prior to any visible commencement of work or furnishing of materials.	Yes
Oregon	No priority can be obtained.	
Penn.	Yes, by prior recordation of mortgage.	Yes
Rhode Island	Priority based on prior recordation.	Yes
South Carolina	Yes. Priority may be obtained by recording a mortgage prior to any visible commencement of work or furnishing of materials.	Yes
South Dakota	Yes. Mortgage must be recorded prior to time first item of material or labor is furnished on the premises, and prior to filing of any notice by the lienholder.	See below.
Tennessee	Filing for record of deed of trust prior to time any materials were delivered to property or any labor expended thereon.	Yes. (See *Kemp v. Thurmond*, 521 S.W. 2d 806-Supreme Ct. of Tenn., March 31, 1975)
Texas	Yes, but only on the land—not on any buildings or improvements constructed on the land. Priority may be obtained by recording mortgage prior to commencement of work or furnishing of materials but the priority applies to the land only and mechanics' and materialmen's liens when perfected are superior to all liens and mortgages as respects the improvements on the land. The rules and	Yes

(*continued*)

145

STATE	CAN A MORTGAGE PRIORITY OBTAIN PRIORITY OVER SUBSEQUENTLY FILED MECHANICS' LIENS, AND, IF SO, HOW?	ARE OBLIGATORY ADVANCES REQUIRED TO OBTAIN PRIORITY?	WILL FILED LIENS TAKE PRIORITY OVER SUBSEQUENT ADVANCES (I.E., REGARDLESS OF ITS OBLIGATORY NATURE, WILL AN ADVANCE MADE AFTER THE FILING OF A MECHANICS' LIEN BE INFERIOR TO SUCH LIEN)?
	regulations as set forth by the Commissioner of Insurance of the State of Texas prohibit giving any mechanic's lien coverage when insuring titles in this state.		
Utah	Yes. Mortgage must be recorded prior to commencement of work or furnishing of material.	Yes, but cases on "obligatory" nature of advances are confusing.	Not if the subsequent advances are obligatory.
Vermont	Priority based on prior recordation. If mortgagee shall receive written notice that any mechanic's lien is to be claimed, such liens shall take precedence over such mortgage as to all subsequent advances made to the mortgagor *except* such advances as the mortgagee may show were actually expended in completing the building.		
Virginia	No priority can be obtained.		
Washington	Yes. Priority may be obtained by recording a mortgage prior to any visible commencement of work or furnishing of materials.	Yes	No
West Virginia	Recordation prior to commencement of work.	Statute is silent.	

Wisconsin	Yes. Priority may be obtained by recording a mortgage prior to any visible commencement of work or furnishing of materials.	Yes
Wyoming	No priority can be obtained.	
Puerto Rico	No mechanics' liens.	No

Since mechanic's lien statutes are subject to legislative whim and judicial interpretation the answers set forth on the chart may not be 100% correct. The information is furnished for use as a convenient guide and *under no circumstances* should the answers set forth be taken as definitive with regard to any particular question of priority.

8
The Permanent Take-Out Commitment

FORMS OF TAKE-OUT COMMITMENTS

The second section of chapter 1 (p. 7) briefly described the new forms of construction loan take-outs. To reiterate, these new forms consist of (1) interest rate adjusted mortgages; (2) mortgages with additional interest provisions; (3) land purchase leasebacks; (4) partnership interests including mortgage/equity combinations; and (5) 100% equity purchases in the form of prebuys. To a large extent though, the drop in inflation and abundance of available capital have made these new forms obsolete and we are slowly seeing a return to the conventional mortgage. Nonetheless, inflation may reappear and circumstances can change once again putting in vogue these new forms of investment, each of which has its own impact upon construction lenders, which must adjust their practices accordingly.

Interest Rate Adjusted and Additional Interest Mortgages

The new interest rate adjusted mortgages and mortgages with additional interest provisions, variations of which have been around for some time, have a minimal effect upon the construction lenders since basically they all follow the format of the conventional mortgage except for the interest and prepayment provisions. The interest rate adjusted mortgages consist mainly of short maturity loans or rollover mortgages, variable rate mortgages with periodic rate adjustments, renegotiable rate mortgages with right of prepayment and graduated payment mortgages. The additional interest provisions include the traditional "kicker" as well as shared appreciation mortgages and convertible mortgages.

Land Purchase Leasebacks

Land purchase leasebacks have also been around for quite some time. They are combined typically with mortgage loans on the improvements. To the extent the land purchase leasebacks resemble a mortgage, no new challenges are faced by the construction lender. To the extent they resemble a true equity, as will be seen, substantial challenges must be confronted.

Partnership Interests

The change in the form of take-out commitment that has created the most difficulties for the construction lender involves the taking of a partnership interest in the property by the otherwise permanent lender. This is accomplished by way of a pure equity partnership (joint venture) or a first mortgage loan plus an equity interest (mortgage-equity combination). In either case, the technique is new and fraught with complications, for although long-term lenders have traditionally entered the equity field, they have done so in the past as sole purchasers of existing properties. Rarely, until today, have we seen this new form of ownership evolving whereby the developer sells a portion of the equity interest in a property to the lender in lieu of long-term financing capital that otherwise would be available. From the construction lender's viewpoint, instead of just having to satisfy the requirements of the permanent loan commitment, it must now not only satisfy similar requirements, but must also await the coming together as partners of two diverse parties, the borrower and the provider of long-term capital, each of which views the property from a different perspective and has traditionally different approaches to the management of a property. Consequently, there is a much higher risk that the take-out commitment will fall apart prior to completion of construction. This places a greater burden on the part of the construction lender to insure that the joint venturers have, in fact, agreed on the basics of their deal prior to opening the construction loan.

Prebuys

Prebuys, where a party commits to purchase a property upon completion of construction, thereby affording take-out funds for the construction loan, offer their own set of unique problems for the construction lender. Since the borrower/developer will no longer have any interest in the property after completion of construction, there is a great tendency to cut corners on actual construction, with the savings pocketed by the borrower/developer. The danger is that corners will be cut to such a degree that the take-out purchase commitment will be jeopardized. In these situations, the construction lender must take extra care that the construction proceeds are advanced for construction strictly in accordance with the approved plans and specifications.

Conventional Mortgages

We are once again seeing the fixed-rate conventional mortgage, which not very long ago was pronounced "dead" by many leaders in the real estate field. These mortgages are not the 30-year self-amortizing type that had previously been prevalent, but instead run for shorter terms of 5-12 years with interest only over the first few years (up to 5 years) and thereafter amortization based upon a 25-30-year basis. Another major difference from the fixed-rate mortgages that prevailed in the past is that most of the new conventional mortgages are not the outcrop of forward commitments, but instead are committed and placed at the time a property is completed (so-called bullet loans). Thus, although the type of mortgage itself is familiar to the construction lender and generally offers no unique problems, the instance in which the take-out commitment becomes viable offers no help to the construction lender looking for a take-out prior to closing the construction loan. However, it seems that as inflation continues to recede and investment capital becomes more available, we will be seeing longer terms on these conventional mortgages and possibly forward commitments as well.

THE TAKE-OUT COMMITMENT FROM THE VIEW OF THE CONSTRUCTION LENDER

This section constitutes a clause-by-clause analysis of the takeout.

A CONSTRUCTION LENDER LOOKS AT PERMANENT LOAN COMMITMENTS*

Most construction lenders will not enter into a loan transaction with a borrower unless the borrower has obtained a permanent "takeout"

---

*This section is reprinted by permission from the Real Estate Review, Vol. 10, No. 2, Summer 1980, Copyright © 1980, Warren, Gorham and Lamont, Inc., 210 South Street, Boston, Mass. All Rights Reserved.

THE PERMANENT TAKE-OUT COMMITMENT 151

loan commitment from a reputable financial institution (or at the very least, a "standby" commitment). The loan called for by the permanent commitment will provide the necessary funds to pay off the construction loan when the project is completed; hence, its availability and validity is of utmost importance to the construction lender. The construction lender must carefully analyze the terms of the permanent loan commitment to assess the likelihood that the permanent lender's preconditions to disbursement will be met prior to the commitment's expiration date and to allow the construction lender to take whatever contingency measures are necessary to insure the borrower's compliance with the commitment terms.

Material Adverse Change. The provision of the permanent loan commitment that probably troubles construction lenders most is the "material adverse change" clause. All permanent loan commitments have or should have such a clause, which generally provides that in the event of a material adverse change in the borrower's financial condition or the facts upon which the loan was underwritten, the permanent lender may cancel the commitment. Permanent lenders adamantly insist upon this type of provision, making it a risk that construction lenders must accept. The only available protection for the construction lender is to negotiate with the permanent lender a standard by which a "material adverse change" can be measured. For example, a material adverse change could be defined as being a change in the state of facts that is of the same magnitude as the fact that the borrower becomes insolvent, bankrupt, or incapacitated.

Loan Documentation. All permanent loan commitments require that the loan documentation (the note, mortgage or deed of trust, assignment of leases, etc.) be acceptable to the lender and its counsel. This is probably the least onerous requirement from the construction lender's viewpoint because, in many cases, the permanent loan is preclosed at the time the construction loan is closed. Alternately, the construction lender can require that the permanent lender and the borrower agree to the loan documents before the construction loan is closed.

Getting the permanent lender to approve title matters and the survey prior to closing the construction loan is a somewhat different matter. However, as a minimum, the construction lender should require that the permanent lender agree to fund its loan subject to the then existing title exceptions and to approve the survey insofar as it purports to reflect a perimeter metes and bounds description of the property. The permanent lender and borrower should also agree as to the form of the surveyor's certification at the time the commitment is made.

Governmental Rules and Regulations. The borrower obviously cannot satisfy the permanent commitment's requirements that the project comply with zoning and environmental laws and regulations and other applicable governmental rules until the project is completed and has received a certificate of occupancy. This is not to say that the construction lender cannot minimize the risks of these requirements. To begin with, preconstruction approval by the municipality of the proposed plans and specifications and the issuance of a building permit should go a long way in assuring that if the planned structure is completed as proposed, it will comply with local law. (The municipality can always reverse itself; however, such an eventuality is unlikely.) A certification from the architect of record and/or local counsel as to compliance is also necessary.

The construction lender should see to it that the permanent lender specifies the form of evidence it will need in order to satisfy itself that the requirements for compliance with governmental rules are satisfied. Typically, the permanent lender requires an opinion from the borrower's counsel or the architect of record, plus final approvals from the various governmental agencies, including the issuance of a final certificate of occupancy. (A temporary certificate of occupancy may be acceptable under certain circumstances.) The permanent lender may also require an endorsement to its title insurance policy ensuring that the completed project is in compliance with applicable zoning ordinances. If this is the case, the construction lender should satisfy itself that such an endorsement will be available and that the borrower is prepared to pay for any added premium charge.

Completion of Construction. A prerequisite to disbursement under any permanent loan commitment is the completion of construction in accordance with plans and specifications that the lender has approved.

The construction lender should permit no construction on the project to commence until the permanent lender has approved the plans and specifications and any preconstruction reports that the commitment requires. (The commitment may require the permanent lender's prior approval of the architect and engineer, soil reports, etc). In addition, as construction progresses, the construction lender must satisfy itself that the borrower/developer has permitted no deviation from the approved plans and specifications. It must make certain that the permanent lender's stage completion requirements (e.g., foundation certifications) have been satisfied.

Tenant Finish Work/Leases. Some permanent lenders specify that the permanent loan cannot be closed merely upon the completion of a shell building; they require completion of various tenant finish work, or, alternatively, that an escrow be established to ensure that funds will be available for completion of tenant finish work. If a lender requires the completion of tenant work, it will most likely also require that the project achieve a certain rental level before the loan closes. Construction lenders must be particularly wary of these requirements. The construction lender must carefully review the proposed cost breakdown and make certain that in balancing the construction loan, it gives due account to the cost of tenant finish work.

The construction lender must also examine all existing leases and make sure that these leases are acceptable to the permanent lender. If possible, it must require that the developer/borrower consummate major tenant leases that the permanent lender has approved prior to commencement of construction. It should require the permanent lender to approve the borrower's proposed standard form of lease.

Debt Service Escrow. On occasion, permanent lenders, as a precondition to closing the permanent loan, require that the borrower place funds in an escrow to cover permanent loan debt service for a specified period of time. In this case, the construction lender must assure itself that the borrower will have the funds to satisfy the debt service escrow requirement. If the borrower's financial condition and the amount of equity capital it is putting into the project leave the construction lender with any doubt, it may require that the borrower provide additional assurances in the form of cash up front or a letter of credit or certificate of deposit. This type of requirement can be considered only on a loan-by-loan basis.

Guarantees. In lieu of and/or in addition to a debt service escrow, some permanent loan commitments ask the borrower to make available personal or corporate guarantees at the time of loan closing. These may be guarantees of repayment of the indebtedness or of completion of tenant finish work. The construction lender's initial risk is that the guarantor will become insolvent. This would be a material adverse change under the permanent loan commitment.

A further risk is that the guarantor will refuse to enter into the guarantee agreement at the appropriate time. Very little can be done about alleviating either risk. However, the construction lender's exposure is not really as great as it might seem. In fact, it is often quite small. When the guarantors for the permanent loan are also guarantors for the construction loan, the construction lender has ample opportunity to review the guarantors' financial statements and determine whether the guarantors will be able to fulfill their obligations when the permanent loan is ready to close. If the permanent loan guarantors and the construction loan guarantors are different, the construction lender can always require as a condition of its loan that the borrower submit for its approval satisfactory financial statements on the permanent loan guarantors.

It is probably impossible to persuade the guarantors of the permanent loan to enter into guarantee agreements at the commencement of the construction loan. The guarantors resent executing a document that relates to a loan not yet in existence. Furthermore, it is debatable whether such a guarantee would be enforceable if it were not reaffirmed when the permanent loan is actually made. (It would be surprising if the permanent lender did not call for reaffirmation.) What the construction lender can do is to require permanent loan guarantors to either execute the permanent loan commitment or otherwise acknowledge in writing their commitment to guarantee the permanent loan.

If the guarantors for the permanent loan and the construction loan are the same, it is probably not necessary for the construction lender to do anything. If the guarantors refuse to guarantee the permanent loan, the construction lender can always enforce the construction loan

THE PERMANENT TAKE-OUT COMMITMENT   155

guarantee, leaving the guarantors no choice but to execute the permanent loan guarantee and substitute a contingent liability for a present one.

Master Lease.   Sometimes, the guarantee that the permanent lender requires takes the form of a master lease. A master lease, unlike a guarantee agreement, can be executed at the time the construction loan is ready to close and still remain effective. Although the term of the lease will not commence until the permanent loan closes, the lease will be a valid and enforceable agreement when executed. The borrower should obtain the permanent lender's approval of the lease form in order to preclude any later disagreements.

Fees.   Most, if not all, permanent lenders require that the borrower pay a commitment fee at the time that the permanent lender issues its commitment. On occasion, the permanent lender may require the borrower to pay additional fees in installments during the time the commitment is outstanding. The construction lender must assure itself that the borrower has paid fees or has sufficient funds to ensure that payments will be made as they fall due.

Other Requirements.   The construction lender must take cognizance of other prerequisites to disbursement that are required by the permanent loan commitment. For example, if the permanent commitment requires a spur track agreement to be in force, the construction lender must look into the availability of such an agreement and, if possible, have its form approved by the permanent lender. If the commitment requires that the borrower/developer have an elevator maintenance contract or other agreements relating to the property, the construction lender must be concerned with their feasibility.

Buy-sell or Tripartite Agreement.   An additional condition of most permanent loans (and construction loans as well) is that the permanent lender, construction lender, and the borrower all enter into an agreement concerning the disposition of the construction loan during and upon completion of construction. This agreement is commonly referred to as a "buy-sell" or "tripartite" agreement. Usually, it must be executed no later than the date of the initial construction loan advance. In order to preserve the validity of the permanent commitment, the construction lender should work with the borrower and permanent lender to have this agreement executed in a timely manner.

Letter of Assurances. Since most buy-sell agreements are based on the permanent lender's standard form, the construction lender should supplement this agreement with what is commonly referred to as "a letter of assurances." The contents of this letter may be incorporated into the buy-sell agreement. However, more often, the permanent lender delivers a separate letter to the construction lender at the same time that the buy-sell agreement is executed. If drafted properly, the letter of assurances contains all of the approvals and agreements by the permanent lender that we have discussed above. At the very least, it should confirm that the permanent loan commitment is in full force and effect, all fees due thereunder have been paid, and that the commitment is free from default on the borrower's part. The remainder of the letter is subject to negotiation.

Conclusion. The construction lender should take the position that the borrower must fulfill all the requirements of the permanent loan commitment that it can satisfy at the time the construction loan is ready to close as a prerequisite to receiving construction loan disbursements. The construction lender should then establish the requirements of the permanent loan commitment that cannot be satisfied at the time the construction loan is ready to close. It should then determine what assurances, if any, it can obtain that these permanent loan requirements will be met in a timely manner. No prescribed formula can be established to fit all permanent loan commitments since the facts of each loan will invariably be different. The construction lender must study the particulars of each transaction and react accordingly.

No matter what safeguards the construction lender establishes, there is no substitute for good underwriting. A construction lender should not rely solely upon a permanent loan takeout commitment for assurance that its loan will be repaid. The construction lender that does so is gambling with its investment.

The substance of the foregoing article is still relevant regardless of the form of the take-out commitment; that is, whether it be some variation of loan commitment, an equity commitment or a combination mortgage/equity commitment. The conditions for the provider of take-out financing to lend money to the borrower or purchase the property must still be scrutinized carefully by the construction lender and the risks inherent in such conditions not being met minimized to the extent possible.

THE BUY-SELL OR TRIPARTITE AGREEMENT

This section, cowritten by the author and Lloyd H. Reed, Vice President, Real Estate Investment Counsel, The Mutual Life Insurance Company of New York, sets forth the construction lender's and permanent lender's view of the buy-sell or tripartite agreement.

THE BUY-SELL OR TRIPARTITE AGREEMENT*

In a real estate transaction, the buy-sell or tripartite agreement is an agreement between the construction lender, permanent lender, and borrower concerning the status of the permanent loan commitment and the disposition of the construction loan during and upon completion of construction.

With the buy-sell agreement, the construction lender closes its loan using loan documents approved and assignable to the permanent lender (other than the building loan agreement and other documents relating solely to the period of construction). The permanent loan is considered "pre-closed" at the time the construction loan closes and the buy-sell agreement is executed. With the tripartite agreement, the permanent loan is not "pre-closed," and the construction lender uses loan documentation applicable only to the construction loan. However, in the agreement, the construction lender agrees to look to the permanent loan commitment as the source for repayment of its construction loan.

*This section is reprinted from *Mortgage Banker* (now entitled *Mortgage Banking*) magazine, with permission from The Mortgage Bankers Association of America. Copyright © Volume 41, Number 3 December 1980.

Whether it is buy-sell or tripartite, the agreement generally serves the purposes of both the construction and permanent lenders, and its execution is usually a requirement of both the constructon loan commitment and the permanent loan commitment.

Construction Lender's View. From the view of the construction lender, the buy-sell or tripartite agreement (hereinafter referred to collectively as the "agreement") constitutes further assurance that the permanent lender intends to honor its commitment to the borrower, resulting in the purchase and/or "take-out" of the construction loan upon completion of construction.

These assurances, welcome as they may be to the construction lender, are by their very nature limited since they are conditioned upon the requirements of the permanent loan commitment being met in a timely manner. To broaden the scope of these assurances, the agreement should contain a statement by the permanent lender indicating which of its commitment requirements have been satisfied to date. Until the construction lender is assured that the permanent loan commitment remains in full force and effect with all conditions capable of being satisfied "signed off" by the permanent lender, the construction loan is not ready to be closed.

To further broaden the scope of these assurances, the permanent lender should assert in the agreement that it has approved the existing state of title and any exceptions thereto, e.g., leases, mineral reservations, etc., as well as the current survey. Approval of any other available items required by the permanent commitment, e.g., leases, should also be obtained if possible, with the objective of minimizing the possibility that the permanent loan commitment requirements will not be met at the time the permanent loan is ready to close.

Despite the best efforts of the construction lender, there will always be requirements of the permanent loan commitment that must await completion of construction. A well drafted agreement will cover some of these requirements by defining what will be necessary in order to comply to the satisfaction of the permanent lender. For example, if the permanent loan commitment requires evidence that the completed building is in compliance with all governmental rules and regulations, the agreement could provide that this provision will be satisfied upon submission to the permanent lender of a final certificate of occupancy. The submission should be accompanied by an opinion of borrower's counsel in a form acceptable to all parties concerned. This opinion is then attached as an exhibit to the agreement.

From the construction lender's vantage point, the agreement should contain an additional provision assigning the borrower's rights in the permanent loan commitment to the construction lender and granting the construction lender the right to cure any defaults of the borrower in complying with the conditions of the permanent loan commitment.

Permanent Lender's View. The permanent lender's view of the agreement differs markedly from that of the construction lender. To the permanent lender, the agreement is a means to assure the acquisition of the investment for which its commitment has been issued. It covers the period of 18 months to two or more years between the issuance of the commitment and the closing of the loan. During this time, economic conditions and interest rates may change drastically, and it may be to the borrower's advantage to look elsewhere for more favorable loan terms. This, of course, is particularly true if the commitment is issued during a period of high interest rates, and there is an expectation that rates may decline. To the permanent lender, then, the purpose, and only purpose, of the agreement is to ensure delivery of the loan at such time as the requirements of its commitment have been met.

A key element to the closing of the permanent loan is the satisfaction of the permanent loan commitment requirements as those requirements are spelled out in the commitment accepted by the borrower. In drafting the agreement, it is not unusual for construction lenders to attempt to seek relief from the permanent loan requirements that they regard as onerous. Indeed, it is rare for a construction lender not to attempt to try to limit or vary the so-called "adverse change" clause and substitute performance by the construction lender for that of the borrower or to make other changes that help lock the permanent lender into taking the construction loan off its hands. The permanent lender generally resists such attempts. Its deal with the borrower has already been fully negotiated; the agreement is no place to reopen negotiations.

This is not to say that the permanent lender can or should be completely inflexible. There is no reason, for example, not to acknowledge that commitment conditions capable of being met have, in fact, been met, assuming such is the case. It is also reasonable for the permanent lender to examine and give preliminary approval to title exceptions, legal description, and surveys. The same is true of leases if, in fact, a lease has been entered into at so early a date.

Perhaps the main thing the construction lender, permanent lender, and borrower can agree upon in the agreement is the form of loan documents. While the permanent lender must reserve the right to require new documents or at least the right of modification of the construction lender's documents for its loan, it is becoming increasingly common for the parties to agree that the permanent lender will take the construction loan papers by assignment upon the completion of construction and closing the permanent loan.

Both lenders can benefit by doing this. The construction lender has assurance that there will be no dispute between the permanent lender and borrower over documents at the time the construction lender is expecting repayment. The permanent lender knows that if the loan papers are already executed, there is less opportunity for the borrower to walk from the commitment should interest rates decline. The borrower also benefits since it must pay the attorneys' fees, filing fees, and taxes for the recording of the documents whether one set or two sets are used. In some states, the fees and taxes can be quite substantial. There is some risk to the permanent lender, chiefly the chance that the construction loan documents may be tainted by usury in these days of high interest rates. However, careful monitoring of interest, fees, and charges received by or on behalf of the construction lender, together with the estoppel of the borrower, can minimize this risk. A deliberate default by the borrower is also a possibility but an unlikely one.

Conclusion. It is apparent from the foregoing that the buy-sell or tripartite agreement benefits all parties involved in the loan transaction. However, each of these parties, the construction lender, the permanent lender, and borrower, has its own interests and concerns that must be protected and safeguarded in the agreement. These conflicting interests should be reconciled in order for the agreement to be entered into and for the parties to derive sufficient benefits from it to make its execution worthwhile.

Borrower's View

The previous section presents two differing views of the buy-sell or tripartite agreement. However, there is yet a third view, that of the borrower. Generally, borrowers look at this agreement as just one more loan document required by the lenders. However, by examining the respective advantages of the agreement to the two lenders, some very real benefits and detriments to the borrower can result.

To a large extent, the advantages to the borrower of the buy-sell or tripartite agreement are similar to those derived by the construction lender. In fact, many borrowers who have been unsuccessful in "pinning down" the permanent lender, welcome the requirements of the construction lender regarding receipt of certain assurances concerning the status of the permanent commitment. A few borrowers have even been known to add a few items to the construction lender's list in order to get a response from the permanent lender. Then, too, the borrower is looking to lock the permanent lender into its commitment as firmly as possible and looks to the buy-sell as one more means of doing so. The main drawback is that this is a two-way street and the borrower also gets "locked in." Should long-term rates decline, many borrowers would be more than happy to walk away from the permanent commitment, leaving the paid commitment fees behind in order to procure a lower rate take-out (this, of course, assumes that permanent lenders will settle for receipt of the commitment fee and not seek other damages, including specific performance).

Prebuys

When the form of take-out financing consists of a commitment or an agreement to purchase the property upon completion, the buy-sell agreement is simply inapplicable since there is no mortgage to assign. In these instances, the construction lender should look to a letter of assurances from the equity purchaser similar to that required of the permanent lender. Most prospective purchasers will be cooperative in this regard since they realize that the construction lender needs these assurances as a precondition to closing the construction loan, and that without the construction loan proceeds there will be no funds to complete the building, which is itself a precondition to the prospective sale and purchase.

9
Loan Administration

SELECTED PROBLEMS

Most of the risks inherent in construction lending will be eliminated by sound loan underwriting and proper legal documentation. The closing of the construction loan marks the beginning of the period when loan administration becomes the critical factor in avoiding the remaining risks faced by the construction lender. During construction the lender is exposed to several potential problem areas, such as the failure to complete the improvements in accordance with the approved plans and specifications; undelivered documentations or acquittances which were not finalized at the closing; delays caused by circumstances beyond the control of the borrower or contractor; and the actual construction.

Failure to Complete the Improvements in Conformity With the Approved Plans and Specifications

The borrower's failure to complete the improvements in conformity with the approved plans and specifications is probably the biggest single problem faced by construction lenders. Such a failure jeopardizes the take-out commitment and/or may put the construction lender in the position of having to advance funds into the project in excess of those originally committed. To avoid and/or minimize this exposure, actual construction must be closely monitored and the loan must always be "in balance"; that is, there should always be sufficient funds available and accounted for to complete the project within the projected cost estimates based upon the percentage of completion to date. In this regard, no loan advance should be approved without an on-site inspection by the lender's representative, usually the inspecting architect, to confirm the proper application of funds disbursed to date and the adequacy of the work in place. Each item of the borrower's payment certification should be gone over by the loan administrator on a line-by-line basis. Preferably, this inspection procedure should be coordinated with that of the provider of take-out funds and in no event should the percentage of the total loan advanced to date and the percentage advanced as against each line item exceed the overall percentage of completion and the percentage of work completed for each such line item.

Careful monitoring of advances will reveal any adjustments in the project budget not otherwise communicated to the lender. If minor increases in costs are involved, they can probably be covered by transfers from the contingency reserve. If more significant cost increases are called for, the borrower should be required to infuse more of its own cash equity into the project to keep the loan in balance.

Fast Track Construction. When the fast track method of construction is being used there are, of course, no preapproved final plans and specifications. In this situation, the loan administrator should be sure to review final plans and specifications for each phase of construction *before* it is commenced and to make sure that such plans and specifications are acceptable to its architect/engineer, the inspecting architect and to the provider of take-out funds.

Open Items After Closing

It is not always practical to require all the i's to be dotted or the t's to be crossed before the construction loan closes. In these situations, it becomes imperative for the loan administrator to set up a tickler system so that all open items are satisfied within specified time frames. Failure to do so could hold up responding to payment requests. Should the open items consist of unexecuted construction contracts, the delay possibly would result in increased construction costs.

Construction Contracts. When the executed construction contracts are finally received, they must be checked against each line item in the budget for the category involved. Lower actual costs than reflected in the budget will result in an increased contingency amount. Higher actual costs, depending on the degree, will either result in a lower contingency amount or a request to the borrower for additional equity capital.

Bonding. If changes in the budget are in fact reflected in the executed contracts or subsequently arise for any other reason, the loan administrator must be cognizant of the requirements of any surety on existing bonding. If the surety requires notification of any changes in the budget, the loan administrator must provide such notice promptly and in writing so as not to jeopardize the validity of the bonds.

Interest. One item which can almost never be finalized at closing is the amount of the interest reserve established in the budget. This is because construction loan interest rates are usually tied to the prime rate, which changes from time to time, and will be affected by changes in the construction schedule. Consequently, the interest reserve must be recalculated on a periodic basis (usually monthly) and if a significant increase is called for, the borrower should be obliged to provide the additional capital by the terms of the loan agreement.

Delays Caused by Circumstances Beyond the Control of the Borrower or Contractor

Acts of God, unusually prolonged inclement weather, material shortages, strikes or other circumstances beyond the control of the borrower or contractor can delay the timely completion of a project. These delays can cause havoc with the projected interest reserve, but more important, can jeopardize the existence of the take-out commitment unless it contains force majeure provisions. However, it is incumbent upon the loan administrator to verify that the provider of take-out funds has been notified of the delays and that a written extension of the take-out commitment has been received.

Actual Construction

The actual construction of the property can also give rise to problems that, at least initially, must be dealt with by the loan administrator. These problems may be caused by disputes with subcontractors and/or suppliers, resulting in liens being filed against the property. They may also result from disputes between the provider of take-out funds and the developer. (The question of liens being filed against the property is covered extensively in chapter 7.) Suffice it to say here that as soon as the loan administrator is aware of any disputes with subcontractors and/or suppliers, an explanation of the cause for such disputes should be sought and if the matter is not promptly resolved, the lender's attorney should be consulted and appropriate remedial action instituted.

Disputes between the provider of take-out funds and the developer may be more difficult to resolve and can be of much greater significance to the construction lender if they give cause for termination of the take-out commitment. In these situations, the loan administrator should do everything possible to reconcile such differences and possibly take remedial action under the construction loan documents if possible. The "right to cure" provisions contained in a buy-sell or tripartite agreement can also be very helpful here, and the importance of having a clear understanding among the borrower and the two lenders spelled out in the tripartite agreement cannot be overemphasized.

THE ROLE OF THE INSPECTING ARCHITECT DURING LOAN ADMINISTRATION

The inspecting architect basically serves as the construction lender's on-site eyes and ears during the construction period by keeping track of the developer's plans and progress. He bears the primary responsibility for determining whether (1) the project is being constructed in accordance with the approved plans and specifications; (2) construction is being diligently pursued and (3) the periodic payment certifications submitted by the borrower are representative of work completed to date.

To determine whether construction is proceeding in accordance with the approved plans and specifications, the inspecting architect must make periodic field inspections to review construction methods and field operations. He must also review test reports covering such matters as concrete strength, soil compaction and field welding. These reviews are in addition to those being conducted by the architect of record, the local building inspector and the representatives of the borrower and the provider of take-out funds.

During his inspections, the inspecting architect should take cognizance of the number of men actually working on the project, the material flow and the general conduct of the parties involved. Measuring actual progress against the initial completion schedule will alert the inspecting architect to the need, if any, for corrective measures to be taken by the general contractor.

Perhaps the most important function of the inspecting architect during the construction phase of the project is to determine whether there are sufficient funds remaining in the undisbursed portion of the loan, and/or available through letters of credit, or other equity funds left on deposit with the construction lender, to complete the work. This is accomplished by comparing the progress made trade by trade, as noted during the actual inspection, with the borrower's payment request certifying work completed up to the time of the inspection. It is primarily for this reason that construction lenders' require the borrower's payment certification to be approved and signed off on by the inspecting architect.

During construction, the inspecting architect is also often consulted by the construction lender regarding any problems that may arise directly relating to construction. The most common occurring problems relate to payment for materials stored on site, retainage and cost overruns.

Construction lenders differ in their treatment of materials not yet in place. Some lenders, fearful of their increased exposure in the event of a failure by the developer, absolutely prohibit payment for any materials unless they are physically installed in the project. Other lenders take a more flexible approach and will advance funds for materials only provided the materials are guaranteed by the manufacturer to meet all specifications, title to the materials is in the name of the borrower and the materials are insured against loss or damage and are either kept in a bonded warehouse or stored on-site under 24-hour guard.

The tricky question arises when the lender is asked to advance funds for materials not yet delivered. This is to insure priority delivery and/or a less expensive price. In times of shortages, slow deliveries and rising cost factors, such payments may be justified. At other times they may not be and the advice of the inspecting architect may be instrumental in such determination.

Sometimes this problem is circumvented by banks lending the borrower funds to cover material purchases through the bank's commercial loan department. When the materials are installed in the project, additional funds are advanced under the construction loan and used to pay off the commercial loan.

Construction lenders also differ in the amount of retainage they require. Typically, conservative lenders will withhold 10% of all requested advances and keep it until construction is completed. Rarely will there be no retainage at all; however, lenders may agree to reduce the amount withheld after a certain percentage of construction completion is attained (typically 50%) or release the retainage as to specified trades when all of the work called for by such trades is completed. The practices vary widely, but in almost all instances, the inspecting architect will be asked to comment on the percentage of completion and whether in fact the specified trades have completed their work. The inspecting architect will also be asked to comment on any "punch list" items at the time of final completion to determine whether release of all or part of the retainage is justified.

Rapidly rising construction costs have led in the past to substantial cost overruns which have placed many projects in jeopardy. Lower inflation should help to alleviate this problem, but lenders can ignore the possibility of increased costs only at their peril. The inspecting architect should be asked to verify construction prices in the property locale prior to acceptance of the construction budget; and, by careful examination of the borrower's payment certification as related to field progress, the inspecting architect should also be in a position reasonably to predict whether difficulties should be expected.

THE ROLE OF THE LENDER'S ATTORNEY DURING LOAN ADMINISTRATION

It has been noted that when the construction loan closes the period of loan administration begins. However, someone must notify the loan administrator that the closing has taken place. This task usually falls to the construction lender's attorney. In fact, the construction lender's attorney typically inaugurates the loan administration period by preparing and distributing a closing report immediately following the closing. This closing report should set forth the salient facts of the loan and be sufficiently detailed to enable the loan administrator and the lender's accounting staff to be familiar with the transaction. A form of closing report, set up as a checklist and containing the pertinent information typically furnished by the lender's attorney, appears at the end of this subsection. The items listed are by no means all-inclusive since other information sought by the lender's personnel relating to the construction loan will be ascertained and readily available from other sources.

During actual construction, the lender's attorney will often be asked to review the status of title prior to each draw request being honored and assure the lender that there are no legal impediments to delay disbursement. Usually, this will entail the procurement of an endorsement to the lender's title insurance policy which updates the policy to a current date and which should indicate whether there have been any intervening liens since the date of the last disbursement. If any liens do appear of record, they should be investigated and depending upon the nature and extent of the loan, remedial action may have to be taken.

Between disbursement, the lender's attorney will also be called upon from time to time to approve proposed easements and rights of way relating to the property and will often be asked to comment upon leases that the borrower desires to enter into.

Of course, if circumstances change and modifications in the construction loan are required, either through choice or as a result of a workout, the construction lender's attorney will be needed to draft revised or amended documents and to coordinate the changes in the legal documentation with the attorney for the provider of take-out funds. In the case of a workout, the construction lender's attorney may be asked to get more deeply involved from the outset and to participate actively in the negotiations.

CLOSING REPORT

TO: Loan Administrator

FROM: Lender's Attorney

RE: Lender's Loan No. _____, Property Address: _____

(1) TOTAL AMOUNT OF LOAN:
(2) PARTICIPATION:
(3) BORROWER:

(4) GUARANTOR: (with joint and several liability for repayment of indebtedness and completion of construction)

(5) BILLING ADDRESS OF BORROWER:

(6) TAKE-OUT COMMITMENT:
(7) INTEREST RATE PRIOR TO DEFAULT:
(8) DEFAULT INTEREST RATE:
(9) PAYMENT TERMS:
(10) FEE DUE (OR PAID) LENDER:
(11) MINIMUM INTEREST RATE:
(12) MAXIMUM INTEREST (OR LEGAL) RATE:
(13) METHOD OF INTEREST CALCULATION:
(14) SERVICING AGENT, IF ANY:
(15) SERVICING FEE:
(16) COMMENCEMENT DATE OF LOAN:
(17) MATURITY DATE OF LOAN:
(18) FIRST ADVANCE:
(19) JOURNALIZE INTEREST: YES ☐   NO ☐
(20) SPECIAL RETAINAGE PROVISIONS:
(21) LETTERS OF CREDIT:
(22) OTHER ITEMS:

Dated: _____

SMOOTHING OUT THE MECHANICS OF CONSTRUCTION LOAN ADVANCES

This section discusses many of the problems confronting borrowers and lenders during the loan administration period some of which were mentioned in the preceding sections, and suggests methods to alleviate these problems:

SMOOTHING OUT THE MECHANICS OF CONSTRUCTION LOAN ADVANCES*

There are few construction lenders who have not heard the cry from their borrower: "Where is my money?" It is unfortunately typical that problems of administering a construction loan and effecting timely advances appear almost immediately after the loan is opened.

Some of the problems may be caused by the lenders. In their rush to open the loan and fund the first construction advance, lenders frequently waive or postpone timely compliance with certain commitment requirements. They just hope that their borrower will quickly follow up and fulfill these requirements. Unfortunately, borrowers are laggard, and, once the initial advance is made, the lenders' personnel invariably turn their attention to opening new loans rather than to clearing up loose ends on existing loans. Consequently, when the borrower requests a second advance, problems suddenly emerge because the borrower has taken no interim action to bring himself into compliance concerning items on which compliance was postponed at the time of the initial advance. Such lack of compliance may be due to the borrower's lack of initiative, but it may also be the result of the lender's ambivalent instructions, or a combination of both. In any event, the end result is that the borrower screams for his money, the lender fails to put his capital to efficient use, and neither party benefits.

This type of delay can readily be avoided if both parties make a checklist of incomplete and/or postponed items accompanied by a timetable for compliance at the time of the initial advance and if they both assign representatives to follow up on these items immediately.

---

*This section, written by the author, is reprinted by permission from the *Real Estate Review*, Vol. 10, No. 1, Spring 1980, Copyright © 1980, Warren, Gorham and Lamont Inc., 210 South Street, Boston, Mass. All Rights Reserved.

Disbursement Methods

There are two methods of disbursing construction advances. The method that is "safest" from a construction lender's viewpoint is commonly called the "voucher plan." The construction lender that uses this technique makes payments directly to the developer's material suppliers or labormen upon receipt of instructions from the owner and/or contractor that it pay particular invoices. Although use of this technique assures the lender that the funds are applied directly to the project and that materialmen and labormen are paid, the technique is a time-consuming procedure that involves the lender in infinite detail. Most developers also dislike it because it takes away the degree of control they would like to have over their contractor and subcontractors.

The second method of construction advance disbursement involves what are commonly known as "progress payments." The lender makes payments, either directly or through the title insurer, to either the owner/developer or the general contractor at completion of various stages of construction. In turn, the developer or contractor pays the subcontractors and possibly the materialmen. Although this is the usual technique of disbursements, it is the source of the many problems that comprise the substance of this article.

Prerequisites to Progress Payments

After making the initial advance, lenders usually require that in order for developers to receive additional construction advances, they must, in each instance, apply for payment. Usually the application must be accompanied by a certification from the inspecting architect and possibly the general contractor. The borrower's application should include a breakdown of the hard and soft costs of the work that has been completed to date; it must also itemize the work to be completed. The architect's certification should state that the improvements that have been completed to date conform to the accepted plans and specifications and meet the requirements of all applicable governmental rules and regulations. The architect should certify further that the completed work justifies the amount of the requested advance and that the funds remaining to be disbursed will be sufficient to complete the project within the time limits prescribed by the permanent ("take-out") loan commitment.

The lender also requires the developer to submit paid receipts and lien waivers or releases from subcontractors and materialmen that evidence that the developer has paid the charges for the completed construction. In addition, the developer must submit to the lender a title continuation or (what is more commonly referred to as) a "date down" endorsement from the title company.

In some circumstances, the lender may require the developer to submit at the time of each advance an updated survey that evidences the fact that the completed work does not encroach on adjoining lands. This is probably unusual. Survey reports are usually required only at the time of the first and last advance and at the time the foundation is completed unless it appears that the improvements are dangerously close to the lot lines.

Given the complex requirements that the developer must fulfill when he submits his application for an advance, it is not surprising that the process sometimes involves costly and irritating delays. But the borrower is not always at fault when he fails to comply with the lender's disbursement prerequisites. Normally, once he has completed various stages of construction work, the borrower will do everything possible to obtain funds from the lender so that he can pay the subcontractors and materialmen and keep the project running smoothly. The lender may prevent a smooth-running operation by failing to define its requirements properly at the outset and by failing to adopt consistent and straightforward operating procedures. This lack of communication between lender and borrower may cause particularly distressing delays in the completion of construction advances. Many construction lenders resolve this problem by giving the responsibility for each loan to a single loan administrator (with proper backup in case of vacation or other absence from the office) who enforces standard procedures and who oversees the individual project until its completion. One such procedure may involve requiring the borrower to submit its application and accompanying data well in advance of the desired disbursement date. This leaves sufficient time for the resolution of any differences over the submitted material between lender and borrower.

Responsibilities of the Construction Loan Administrator

A knowledgeable loan administrator is an invaluable asset to a construction lender. The loan administrator should be able to evaluate minor deviations from the usually required information in the borrower's application for an advance and the requisite certifications and make a practical decision whether to proceed with the disbursement despite such technical failures. Often enough, an inexperienced administrator will reject a borrower's application for payment because the application and the certificates were not 100 percent complete, although there were no material omissions. Such an unreasonable decision obviously results in unnecessary delays and inconvenience to all parties concerned. On the other hand, the administrator must be sure that the application or certifications do not reveal significant cost overruns or material omissions.

If such problems exist, they should be identified early and remedied as soon as possible. In those cases, the construction lender is justified in withholding advances until the problem has been worked out to its satisfaction (possibly by requiring additional financing or additional funds from borrower). The construction lender must always be sure that the loan is "in balance" (i.e., that the construction funds remaining after each disbursement are sufficient to complete construction) prior to each advance of additional funds.

Protecting the Lender Against Mechanics' Liens

The lender must insist on receiving paid receipts and lien waivers or releases from subcontractors and materialmen and the "date down" endorsement from the title company so that it is assured that the construction loan proceeds already advanced have actually gone into the project.

Mechanic's lien laws vary from one jurisdiction to another and their local application affects the critical nature of these prerequisites to disbursement.

In a number of states (e.g., New York), mechanic's liens do not present a problem provided the building loan agreement is filed before the construction mortgage is recorded, and the agreement contains a trust fund clause. A trust fund clause gives the advanced funds to the borrower in trust and specifies that the funds must pay for the costs of improvements before they can be used for other purposes. This agreement protects the lender provided that it does not continue to advance funds once a supplier files a mechanic's lien. However, the priority of the lender's advances can be lost if the building loan agreement is modified or if the lender permits the parties to deviate from its terms (e.g., it waives the architect's inspection) without the consent of all parties. The lender will also lose its priority if it participates with the borrower in a diversion of the trust funds (e.g., it permits advanced funds to be used for the payment of a tax lien rather than for construction). Usually, the lender can protect its priority by adhering strictly to the terms of the building loan agreement and by advancing funds only to the borrower; provided, however, that at the time of each advance the lender receives an updated title report indicating that there are no intervening liens. The procurement of this report may, of course, result in delays in effecting advances.

In jurisdictions in which the lender's construction mortgage generally has priority over mechanic's liens, the lender may occasionally advance funds directly to the borrower without awaiting a title report. However, this is a risky procedure and should be undertaken only if the borrower and general contractor have a proven track record and a sound financial base. In addition, if the lender agrees to do this for one advance, it should insist that prior to the next advance the borrower submit the paid receipts and lien waivers or releases along with a title report that evidences that as of the last advance, the subcontractors and materialmen were actually paid, and that no liens were filed. In other words, an exposure of this sort should be limited to a single advance.

In those states where the priority is given to subcontractors and materialmen, the procurement of title insurance protection against mechanic's liens is almost mandatory. In these jurisdictions, lenders would be wise to require that advances be placed in a construction loan escrow controlled by the title company. The title insurer's mechanic's lien coverage in such areas is usually limited to protection against liens arising from work for which payment has been made with funds disbursed by the title insurer (or by the lender with the title insurer's approval). Its insurance cannot protect against liens arising from work for which no payment has been made.

Some title companies may make available initial protection against mechanic's liens for the full amount of the construction loan. However, such protection is costly, and the insurer almost always requires that the title company control the disbursement of the loan proceeds. It should be pointed out that neither form of coverage protects a lender against liens arising from improvements contracted for subsequent to the effective date of the title policy, liens not financed by the proceeds of the particular construction loan, or liens arising from work that the lender is obligated to finance after the date of the title policy.

Disbursing Funds Through the Title Insurer

Frequently, in a situation where the construction advances are being disbursed by the title insurer, there may be a time lag of two to three days between the time that the title insurer receives the funds from the lender and the time it disburses those funds to the borrower or subcontractors and materialmen. During this period, presumably, the title insurer is proceeding at all deliberate speed to "run down" the title in order to see if any intervening liens were filed since the last advance. Possibly the title insurer makes an inspection of the property.

To speed things up, the developer should try to make arrangements with the title insurer at the time the loan is opened, to have the title insurer commence its title preparation when the borrower notifies the insurer that it has forwarded to the lender the prerequisites for an advance (say, the application and architect's certification). Of course, when it makes such an arrangement, the borrower runs the risk that if its application is rejected by the lender, it will have to pay for an unnecessary title rundown.

An alternative technique for speeding up the title insurer's rundown and inspection is for the lender to deposit the funds with the title insurer to accrue interest for the account of the borrower until they are disbursed by the insurer's release. This would remove any incentive the title insurers might have for unnecessarily delaying disbursement. (All title insurers vigorously deny that they delay disbursements unnecessarily, but I have yet to see a title insurer agree to pay interest on monies held for the borrower in this type of situation.)

The lender who transmits funds to the title insurer for the insurer to disburse should make sure that the funds are appropriately received and disbursed. In one horrible example, a lender wired its funds from Boston to a Chicago bank on June 21. The funds were literally lost, and they did not show up in Chicago until July 5. The lender had no follow-up after it wired the funds; it just assumed that the monies would reach the title insurer and be disbursed in the normal course of events. The title insurer was unaware that the funds were on their way and therefore was unaware that they were delayed. The frantic borrower could not reach the lender's loan administrator who was on vacation.

There is no excuse for such extreme inefficiency. Wiring instructions can be set up so that the recipient is aware that funds are in transit and the insurer can be required to notify the lender as soon as it receives the funds. If by the end of banking hours the lender has not received word that the funds have arrived, it is immediately alerted that a problem may exist, and it can take whatever steps are necessary to correct the situation.

The Final Advance

Before it funds the final advance, the construction lender must require evidence that the improvements have been completed in accordance with the accepted plans and specifications and that they are approved for permanent occupancy by all governmental authorities. (A certificate from the inspecting architect and a Certificate of Occupancy are usually sufficient evidence.) In addition, the lender should receive a final as-built survey, a final "date down" endorsement to the title policy, and evidence that the permanent commitment is in full force and effect and any special retainage requirements have been satisfied.

Since the final advance probably includes that proportion of all construction costs that was held back to assure completion of the project (construction retainage is usually at least 10 percent) and/or additional funds that were held back to satisfy special problems (such as, special retainage subject to rental achievement), construction lenders are understandably reluctant to release the final advance until all of the prerequisites have been satisfied. On occasion, the final advance may even be delayed until the funding of the permanent loan. In such situations, the borrower, construction lender, and permanent lender may have to work together to procure the necessary prerequisites that make it possible to issue the final advance and that permit the payoff of the construction loan and the closing of the permanent loan.

CONSTRUCTION LOAN ACCOUNTING

No discussion of loan administration will be complete without reference to construction loan accounting. Interest billings must be computed and checks and balances set up so that the interest collected does not run afoul of any applicable usury provisions. Books and records of advances and other charges must also be kept. Although more and more of this work is being done by computer, the construction lender must still have personnel capable of interpreting the interest related provisions of the loan documents and manually computing many of the loan charges in the event of a computer breakdown or if special information is required.

The bookkeeping function of the lender's accounting staff is fairly straightforward and is in no need of explanation. The analytical role of the accountants is more interesting and desires special mention. Basically, the phrase "garbage in–garbage out" is a familiar one and is particularly applicable here. Unless there is a proper reading of the interest provisions of the Note and other loan documents, the data fed into the computer needed to compute the billings to be sent to the borrower will be insufficient to produce an accurate accounting of what to charge. The loan documents may call for augmented rates of interest under certain circumstances and may differ from loan to loan on the calculation of basic interest. Either from a closing report or directly from the loan documents, the accountants must be made aware of these provisions and be able to interpret and program the information furnished to them.

The interest rates charged on construction loans will usually be floating rates (typically tied to the bank's prime rate) and hence the accountants must also flag any applicable usury ceilings so that the interest charged does not run afoul of the usury limitations. Since interest is generally calculated based upon the 365/360-day method in order to maximize the lender's return, particular care must be taken when the legal interest limit is neared since the effective rate received by the lender may in fact exceed the maximum rate allowable even though the nominal rate charged is within permissible limits. A more detailed discussion of this issue is contained in the following section:

CALCULATION OF INTEREST—LENDERS BEWARE!*

Traditionally, lenders have been concerned with usury limitations only when they considered the contract rate set forth in the loan documents and any incidental fees or charges that they may have collected on the loan. Rarely, if ever, has the lender's method of calculating interest played a part in these deliberations. That is, until recently when the courts in at least two states have held lenders guilty of usury as a result solely of the methods that they used to calculate the interest.

Methods of Calculating Interest. There are three generally recognized methods of calculating interest:

- The 365/365 day method;
- The 360/360 day method (commonly known as the 30/360 method); and
- The 365/360 day method.

365/365 Method. The first method, (365/365), divides the rate of interest by 365 to produce a daily interest factor. When the daily interest is multiplied by the exact number of days in the month and the product is then multiplied by the unpaid principal balance, monthly interest due has been calculated. The formula looks like this:

$$\text{Monthly interest} = \frac{\text{interest rate}}{365} \times \text{exact number of days in month} \times \text{unpaid principal balance}$$

Obviously, this formula produces different interest charges for months with differing lengths.

360/360 Method. The second method, (360/360), divides the rate of interest by 360 to produce a daily interest factor. When the daily interest is multiplied by 30 and the product is then multiplied by the unpaid principal balance, monthly interest due has been calculated. The formula looks like this:

---

*This section, written by the author, is reprinted by permission from the *Real Estate Review*, Vol. 9, No. 4, Winter 1980, Copyright © 1980, Warren, Gorham and Lamont, Inc., 210 South Street, Boston, Mass. All Rights Reserved.

$$\text{Monthly interest} = \frac{\text{interest rate}}{360} \times 30 \times \text{unpaid principal balance}$$

This method treats each month as if it had thirty days: Thus, assuming the unpaid principal balance remains the same, the interest charged each month is the same. In months that have more or fewer than thirty days, the amounts of interest due that result from this calculation differ from the interest charged using the 365/365 method. However, the amount of interest due over a calendar-year will total exactly the same amount for both methods.

365/360 Method. Under the third method, (365/360), the annual rate of interest is divided by 360 to produce a daily interest factor. That daily interest rate is multiplied by the exact number of days in the month, and the product is then multiplied by the unpaid principal balance. The formula is the following:

$$\text{Monthly interest} = \frac{\text{interest rate}}{360} \times \text{exact number of days in month} \times \text{unpaid principal balance}$$

This method appears to be a combination of the first two methods, but it actually results in substantially greater total interest charges over a calendar-year than do the other two methods. This method has led to difficulties in the courts of which lenders must beware.

The Oregon Case. On August 14, 1975, the U.S. Supreme Court let stand a decision holding a bank liable for damages in a usury action because the bank computed interest on a 365/360 basis and thus exceeded the state statutory ceiling on interest.[1] The Court, in rendering its decision, rejected the bank's argument that to calculate interest in another manner would create an undue bookkeeping burden, be against customary lending practices and be generally inconvenient. The Court further asserted that it was not necessary for the bank knowingly to intend to charge a usurious rate. That the bank under-

---

[1] *American Timber Trading Co.* v. *First Nat'l Bank of Ore.*, 334 F. Supp. 888 (1971), *aff'd* 511 F.2d 980 (D.C. Cir. 1973), *cert. denied* (1975).

stood its method of computation was regarded as sufficient knowledge of intent.

Impact. The direct impact of the decision in this case was limited to the interpretation of Oregon law at the time the loan was made. (Oregon has since enacted a statute which limits the defense of usury to transactions involving less than $150,000.) However, the indirect ramifications of the decision go much further, and may be a factor in all those states where there is no statutory provision relating to computation of interest, and the statutory ceiling on interest is the same as the contract rate called for by the loan documents.

Red Flags. After the Supreme Court's action, a number of red flags were waved by the legal profession. For the most part, institutions ignored these warnings mainly because changing their method of calculation was inconvenient and a source of administrative problems, the reasons advanced by the bank in the Oregon case but rejected by the Court.

The Arkansas Case. Unfortunately, a mortgage company in Arkansas was one of many lenders that failed to take cognizance of the Oregon decision, and had its note and mortgage canceled as a result. This 1977 case[2] involved a construction loan bearing interest at 10 percent per annum (the legal limit in Arkansas). The lender had sent computerized monthly statements to the borrower in which interest was compounded and a daily interest factor computed by the 365/360 method. The Court stated that even though the borrower had made no payments under the note and mortgage, the use of the 365/360 method of calculation produced an interest rate that exceeded the legal maximum, and thus the lender was subject to penalties for violation of the Arkansas usury statutes. (The 10 percent $\frac{365}{360}$ produces an annual rate of almost 10.14 percent.) This case was cited for support in a subsequent Arkansas case wherein the Court stated that it was not likely "to overlook a mathematical error when responsibility for the calculation of interest had been assumed by a finance company."[3]

[2]*Cagle v. Boyle Mortgage Co.*, 549 S.W.2d 474 (1977).
[3]*Southland Mobile Home Corp. v. Webster*, 563 S.W.2d 430, 432 (1978).

Conclusion. Notwithstanding the Oregon and Arkansas Court decisions, many lenders continue to calculate interest, using the 365/360 method. In those states that have no statutory ceilings on interest or in which the statutory ceiling is substantially in excess of the interest charged by the lender, lenders should encounter no problems. However, a lender holding a note in which the contract rate of interest is also the legal limit can calculate interest on the basis of the 365/360 method only at its peril.

The lender's accountants must also be made aware of any fees collected on the loan which may be considered additional interest for usury purposes, and instructed on how to account for such fees throughout the loan term.

10
The Problem Loan

FACTORS TO WATCH OUT FOR

Construction Risks

Until a project is completed and the construction loan is paid in full, the construction lender bears all of the risks of construction. These risks may arise out of or be caused by the construction contract; delays in construction; cost overruns including increased building costs; failure to comply with plans and specifications; poor job management; encroachments and protrusions; mechanics' liens; diversion of funds by the borrower or construction contractor; title problems; bankruptcy of the borrower or contractor; marketing problems; certificates of occupancy; zoning problems; building problems; construction insurance; technical/legal problems; lack of funds to complete and loss of or refusal to fund the takeout. The construction lender knowingly accepts these risks but does or should do everything possible to minimize them. This is accomplished by careful underwriting and good loan administration, with a close monitoring of construction costs and progress. However, despite the best efforts of construction lenders, not every project gets properly built for the budgeted amount within the construction time schedule.

Monitoring the Loan

If the construction loan is being administered properly, the loan administrator should be alerted to many of the problems that may arise before they get too serious. The careful monitoring of construction loan draw requests from the borrower (which should be approved by the general contractor and inspecting architect) will disclose the progress of construction, cost factors in relation to the approved budget and compliance with the plans and specifications. Periodic visits to the construction site may also reveal if any general building problems or job management problems exist. If any variations from established practices or previous estimates and approvals are disclosed, explanations should be sought and remedial action taken immediately.

In addition, the loan administrator and/or the lender's counsel, should be receiving periodic title reports with each advance. These reports will indicate if any mechanics' liens have been filed against the property or if any other title problems have arisen since the date of the last title report.

One of the danger signs that lenders should particularly watch out for is a request for loan increases or waivers of conditions. These often precede a workout and necessitate close independent study by the loan administrator.

Unfortunately, many areas are not subject to monitoring and/or hidden factors preclude the lender from being aware of problems before it is too late to inject a "quick fix." In these situations, extensive and quite often laborious workouts may be necessary.

CONSTRUCTION WORKOUTS

Complete Construction

If problems start to develop on a project, the overriding concern of the construction lender must be to have construction completed. Until then, the project is undersecured and the title almost always unmarketable; there is the possibility of losing the take-out commitment and an increased risk of job shutdown, vandalism, loss of contractors and physical deterioration. To minimize these risks, the lender must act quickly and decisively, with due regard for the possibility of waiving or impairing rights the lender has against third parties such as guarantors and title and bonding companies.

Participants in the Workout

All of the parties involved in the construction loan process are potential participants in a workout situation. In addition to the lender's personnel, these parties generally include the borrower or principals of the borrowing entity; the guarantors; the general contractor and sometimes major subcontractors; the inspecting architect; the title company; the provider of take-out funds; major tenants; the bonding company; subordinate lenders; the hazard insurer; construction loan participants and the borrower's personal bank lenders, if any. The nature of the borrower's default and the problems surrounding the loan will determine which of these parties are necessary to procure a successful workout.

Determine Underlying Problems

The determination of the underlying problems will also have a great bearing on the lender's approach to the situation. For example, if economic circumstances create conditions beyond the control of borrower and lender such as interest rates skyrocketing to unforeseen heights which throw the project budget out of line, it is probably best to work with the borrower in solving the problem. However, if the borrower has been diverting funds from the project or simply exercising poor construction management, it may be best to either remove the borrower from the project entirely or at the very least exercise tighter controls over the method and manner of disbursing the construction loan proceeds. Thus, preliminary to any workout it becomes incumbent upon the construction lender thoroughly to assess the difficulties encountered and to make a factual determination as to their cause.

Status of Completion. One of the most important facts to be considered by the lender is the present status of the project. The lender must determine the percentage of completion, whether work is progressing and in accordance with the plans and specifications, whether the quality of the work done to date is sufficient or whether remedial work will be necessary, etc. The answers to these questions will permit a judgment as to the anticipated completion date which, in turn, can be compared to the outside date of the take-out commitment, completion dates in major tenant leases, the building permit expiration date and the anticipated marketing conditions for the project at the time of completion.

Mechanics' Liens. If it is determined that mechanics' liens are a problem, the lenders counsel must carefully review the title policy to determine if the title insurance is effective and whether future advances can be made by the lender without jeopardizing the priority of its first lien. Lenders should take note that liens stemming from circumstances known to the insured and not disclosed are not covered by title insurance. Consequently, if the lender has knowledge of a contractor's notice of claim or is aware of circumstances that may lead to such notices being issued, it is generally best to alert the title insurer to the situation.

Bonds. Similarly, if a payment and performance and/or completion bond is involved, the lender should be aware of any alleged defaults on its part or that of the borrower-owner and that a modification of the construction contract without the surety's consent may serve to release the bond.

Consult With Counsel

Before undertaking any action, the lender should consult with its counsel to determine what rights the lender has against third parties, what defenses there may be to the exercise of these rights and what, if any, legal or regulatory problems may have to be faced before the project can be completed. Generally, if the loan had been properly documented at closing, the lender should have rights pertaining to almost all persons related to the construction process.

Theoretically, the lender should be able to exercise its various assignments of contracts and agreements, step into the shoes of the borrower/developer, and deal directly with the general contractor, architect, engineer, provider of take-out funds, and others, all without additional cost other than that set forth in the original documents entered into between each of the various parties and the borrower. Practically, this is rarely the case. General contractors are not always cooperative, nor are the architects and engineers of record, not to mention the provider of take-out funds who would much rather get out of its commitment once the project encounters difficulties. The attorney for the lender should review all the relevant documents to advise the lender as to what steps must be taken to preserve their viability.

Defenses

The lender and its counsel should also consider the possible defenses the borrower or third parties may raise to the exercise of the lender's rights. These defenses may include usury and doing business requirements, alleged defects in the loan documents, claims of the lender's unreasonableness or delay in approving plans or funding requested advances, and priority claims of mechanics' lienors and/or other third parties.

Many lenders encounter difficulties because they have placed too much reliance on the builder's prior track record in lieu of a thorough underwriting analysis of the particular project. Lenders' counsel often fall into the same trap in the legal and regulatory field, assuming the thoroughness of the developer and his counsel as to such matters as the availability of utilities to the project, access to public roads and easements, compliance with zoning, building code, environmental and other regulatory matters and matters dealing with the state of title and survey exceptions. The assumptions of competence at loan closing must be confirmed when problems arise, and remedial action taken, if necessary.

Feasibility Study

In addition to facing up to the problems that may be encountered in the workout, the lender must also make a feasibility study to determine whether the project justifies further investment. This will entail an independent determination of the cost to complete and the consideration of possible alternative uses for the project; for example, transferring garden apartments into condominiums. The continued or projected availability of take-out funds must also be considered as should the possibility of selling off portions of the project in a real estate syndication to raise additional capital needed to complete.

Options Available to Lender

Once the lender has ascertained the underlying causes for the project's plight, assessed its rights vis-à-vis the borrower and other parties and gauged the economics of the project, it becomes time for the lender to set its objectives and choose between the various options available. These consist basically of the sale of the lender's mortgage to a third party (alternately, the bonding company could take over the project); foreclosure and the pursuit of remedies against the borrower and guarantors; and a workout. Obviously, the first choice is the one most desired by lenders but it is also the least likely to occur. The choice of foreclosure is more viable but will generally translate into a substantial loss for the lender unless construction is in its initial stages and/or the borrower or guarantor is good for a deficiency judgment. Partially completed structures are just not marketable and few bring pro rata value at foreclosure sale.

The workout remains as a chance for the lender to recoup its losses and realize a return of all or substantially all of its investment. As an aside, and provided it is successful, it also serves to redeem the loan officer who approved the loan initially and who generally will be in favor of some sort of workout arrangement rather than abandoning a problem loan. Thus, politics as well as economics often dictate the choice of workout over foreclosure.

Primary Goal

Assuming the lender is willing to work out the loan, it generally has a formidable task ahead of it. Decisions must be made quickly and decisively, rights of and against third parties must be protected and conflicting objectives must be reconciled. The primary goal is to complete construction as soon as possible while at the same time controlling performance of the work done and avoiding day-to-day management decisions. The lender must insure that sufficient funds are available to complete but at the same time minimize its own financial obligations and maximize the financial contribution of other parties. The lender must also insulate the project from bankruptcy stays and mechanics' lien actions and avoid adverse regulatory, tax and doing business aspects of the workout.

There are various alternatives for the achievement of these objectives, not all of which will lead to a successful workout. This puts a premium on lender personnel who have the authority and are able to compromise when needed and act decisively at other times.

Control and Ownership of the Project

One of the first issues that must be resolved in a workout relates to control and ownership of the project during the workout period. When the borrower retains control and ownership, the lender should carefully monitor payments to the general contractor and subcontractors to insure that there is no diversion of funds from the project and a greater control of actual costs. Generally, unless the borrower comes up with additional equity capital to cover the cost overruns, its control and ownership of the project is only a short-run proposition. The lender at some point will be looking to take over the project to recoup its investment or at the very least force a sale to a third party.

If the lender is determined to take direct control and possession of the project, this can be accomplished by consent of all parties without foreclosure and with ownership, at least initially, remaining with the borrower; by the acceptance of a deed in lieu of foreclosure from the borrower; or, by purchasing the property at a foreclosure sale. The first means of gaining control, that is, by consent of all parties without having title to the property, is generally the least attractive to the lender since it would make the lender a "mortgagee in possession," thereby exposing the lender to a strict accountability of its activities with the borrower possibly being the beneficiary of this newly created liability. When the lender and borrower agree that the lender should take over the project, this is best accomplished by means of a friendly foreclosure or a deed in lieu of foreclosure, assuming there are no other adverse interests to contend with. In this way the lender has both control and title to the property.

When adverse interests exist, for example, mechanics' liens and junior mortgages, a friendly foreclosure will not be possible; and, if the borrower is agreeable to furnishing a deed in lieu of foreclosure, the lender should accept same provided it does not have to release its first mortgage lien on the property. This can be accomplished in many jurisdictions by inserting non-merger language in the borrower's deed. The lender will then acquire control and ownership of the project and can proceed to foreclosure its mortgage without interference from the borrower in order to clear up any outstanding title problems and wipe out the mechanics' liens and/or junior mortgages. In most cases, under these circumstances, the borrower will be willing to grant the deed in lieu of foreclosure in consideration for the lender releasing the borrower from any personal liability it may have for repayment of the indebtedness or completion of construction.

When the borrower and lender do not agree on control and ownership of the property, the outcome is usually a contested foreclosure action. In these instances, the lender will or should request the court grant it possession during the foreclosure action or alternatively (and perhaps preferably) to appoint a receiver. Unfortunately, the rules pertaining to the appointment of a receiver vary from state to state and local laws and customs must be observed.

Bankruptcy

Problems arise in the contested foreclosure action when the borrower files in bankruptcy. The ramifications of the borrower's bankruptcy and the resultant stay in the foreclosure proceedings will be taken up in a separate section. However, suffice it to say at this point that filing for bankruptcy or even the threat to file and the consequent delays encountered as a result is oftentimes a weapon used by borrowers to coerce lenders into making concessions that would not otherwise be made. Only by a thorough knowledge of the Bankruptcy Code and of the facts of the particular situation can lenders properly analyze the impact of bankruptcy on the project and determine whether any concessions are warranted to forestall such a result.

Other Factors

The threat of the borrower's bankruptcy is not the only factor that may deter a lender from going through a contested foreclosure, or even taking over the project in a friendly proceeding. Local taxation requirements and "doing business" may be prohibitive, as may be the effects upon the lender of federal and home state taxation. Problems relating to election of remedies and marshaling of assets may arise as may rights of redemption and clogging the equity of redemption. If the lender is a real estate investment trust (REIT), certain management limitations may apply, and for all lenders the effect of taking possession, foreclosing or taking a deed in lieu may have an adverse accounting effect relating to such matters as loan classification, loss reserves and amortization of cost of owned property. REITs are particularly sensitive to the accounting effect of workouts.

Bonding and Title Companies

An additional alternative to lender or borrower control of the project is for the bonding or title company to take over and complete construction. This rarely takes place and will occur only when the obligation of the bonding or title company is so clearly established that they have no choice but to perform. However, lenders must decide whether performance in this manner by the bonding or title company is desirable. Neither entity probably has any expertise in development and although the lender's exposure will be minimized to the extent of funds advanced, this lack of experience in development may put these funds further into jeopardy. In any event, in the case of title insurers at least, they will almost never elect to complete a project, finding it much more preferable to pay off existing claims than tie up their funds and personnel in a workout situation.

Guarantors

There is also the possibility that guarantors will be asked to take over the project and complete construction. However, in most instances, those parties who have guaranteed completion are so related to the borrower, that from the lender's viewpoint they constitute the same entity.

Third Parties

Bringing in a third party to complete is a different story. This involves bringing in an additional party who is willing either to purchase the lender's mortgage, or purchase the borrower's fee interest in the property subject to the lender's mortgage. Since the uncompleted building is most likely undersecured, tax inducements constitute the main incentive for the third party, and the transaction is usually conditioned upon a refinancing of the construction mortgage on terms more favorable to the new owner.

Financing During the Workout

Another issue that needs to be resolved involves financing of the project during the workout period. If the lender takes title to the property, the additional funds invested will be considered equity capital. If the lender desires the funds to be advanced under its mortgage, the alternative is to take title in the name of a nominee and then lend the nominee funds to complete. Advancing funds, except for taxes and any essential repairs or under judicial protection, prior to obtaining title at a foreclosure sale frequently presents priority problems vis-à-vis mechanics' liens.

Should the borrower remain in possession of the property, the construction lender can always infuse additional funds into the project by increasing the amount of the total loan, providing gap or standby financing, deferring, reducing or waiving interest or by simply absorbing a portion of the loss.

Financing arrangements with other parties to contribute funds toward completion can and should be attempted. The title or bonding companies may pay for cost overruns or agree to make gap or standby loans for the construction overage should their liability be established. Subordinate lenders, guarantors or limited parties may also agree to advance extra funds to preserve their interests, either in the form of cash or a letter of credit to gain time in which to have additional capital available upon completion. This can be accomplished via a further syndication (for tax shelter) of the borrower's equity interest in the property or an increase in the amount of the take-out commitment. The possibility of a subordinated sale leaseback to raise additional capital should also be explored.

Implementation of the Workout

Consent of Third Parties. Once the form of workout has been agreed upon, it remains to be implemented and administered. As stated, the need to proceed quickly must be tempered by the necessity of gaining the consent and approval of third parties. If the status of title is to be changed or modifications made to the construction loan agreement or general construction contract, or any changes made in the plans and specifications, the consent of the guarantors, the title insurer and the parties to the buy-sell agreement, which includes the provider of take-out financing, must also be obtained. Failure to procure such consents may result in a waiver of rights against the third parties.

Checks and Balances. The lender should maintain a thorough system of checks and balances regarding future disbursements. These should include the requirement for lien waivers from all subcontractors and suppliers. Facts disclosed may necessitate checks payable jointly to the creditor and the borrower or directly to such creditor. However, and without distracting from the lender's control of financing, the lender must realize that only one entity (the general contractor or equivalent) can have clear responsibility for dealing with subcontractors, utilities companies and local municipalities, and so on, in order for construction to proceed efficiently and for completion to take place as soon as possible. If the parties do not feel that the existing contractor is capable of doing this, the general contract should be terminated and the job rebid. Before doing so, the lender would be well advised to assess the likelihood of inducing a reputable new contractor to finish a partially completed structure, with all the warranty ramifications or whether it would be preferable for the lender to control the work and subcontractors directly or to hire an independent construction management company. The lender's action will to a large extent depend upon the percentage of completion at the time.

Security and Insurance. Until the workout has finally been implemented, the lender should be satisfied that steps have been taken to prevent theft and vandalism at the project and to insure that sufficient builder's risk casualty insurance is being maintained. This may entail posting of 24-hour guards, informing the insurance carriers of the special circumstances relating to the project and procuring endorsements to existing policies.

Legal Documentation. Implementation of the workout will also necessitate numerous changes in legal documentation relating to financing arrangements, change of ownership and/or construction management changes. This will necessitate bringing local counsel and possibly accountants into the implementation stage, if they have not already been a party to the proceedings, and will result in additional costs for the project to the extent of the attorneys' and accountants' fees and expenses.

Administration of the Workout

The most difficult part of any workout for the lenders involves its administration. Most lenders simply do not have the personnel with the proper orientation and time to administer the day-to-day goings on of a workout. This is one significant reason why lenders are generally reluctant to take on this responsibility and attempt to avoid taking direct possession of the property.

Conclusion

The foregoing should highlight the need for careful loan underwriting, detailed documentation evidencing the loan and frequent independent monitoring of construction progress as called for in prior chapters. However, even with such precautions, problems may still arise and lenders should be prepared to take immediate remedial action as soon as any hint of trouble is discovered.

Looking on the bright side in any workout situation, there is always inflation. Due to current high replacement costs, many workouts represent bargain investments, even if the actual cost to complete at the time exceeded the investment value of the property based upon capitalization of the then currently anticipated income. The big question the lender must ask itself is whether the demand and inflation will produce sufficient value over the long haul to justify the expenditure of additional time and money.

BANKRUPTCY AND THE PROBLEM LOAN

It was mentioned in the preceding section that the filing in bankruptcy (or even the threat to file in bankruptcy) by the borrower can have a material impact on a workout situation. This is true for several reasons, the most notable ones being the bankruptcy provisions relating to automatic stays, cramdowns and preferences and fraudulent transfers. In addition, recent court decisions interpreting these provisions have given lender's additional cause for concern when faced with bankruptcy situations.

Automatic Stays

Once a petition in bankruptcy is filed, the immediate effect is a stay on all actions against the debtor with the debtor remaining or put back in possession of the property. The secured creditor (lender) cannot foreclose its lien or seek or continue the appointment of a receiver or do anything else to collect upon the outstanding debt or protect its investment. To obtain relief from the stay, the lender must file a complaint with the bankruptcy court which is obligated to hold a preliminary hearing on the subject within 30 days from such filing. If the hearing is not held within the 30-day period, the stay will automatically be lifted. Relief from the stay will also be granted if it is shown at the hearing that the lender cannot be "adequately protected" if it does not get the property back or that the debtor has no equity in the property and the property is not necessary to an effective reorganization.

The standards of adequate protection established by the Bankruptcy Code relate to economic depreciation of the property and do not necessarily equate to the debt service on the loan. The intent is for the lender to be adequately protected so that it would be in the same position vis-à-vis the value of the property at the time of liquidation than it would have been if it had foreclosed at the commencement of bankruptcy proceedings. This requires a valuation of the property and payment for any economic depreciation in cash or by substitute collateral. If neither is forthcoming or available, the stay will be lifted.

Although it would appear on its face that the property of a single asset debtor is necessary to a reorganization, if the debtor has no equity in the property, the legislative history of the Code indicates that the stay will be lifted. The rationale is that under such circumstances, it would be impossible to have an *effective* reorganization, which is the standard that the Code imposes upon the courts.

If the court rules against the lender at the preliminary hearing, a final hearing must be held within 30 days after the conclusion of the preliminary hearing. This is a relatively short time interval; however, with the exception of a few states (e.g., New York), no outside time for conclusion of the final hearing is established, leaving open the date when the lender will receive a final decision upon its complaint.

Cramdowns

Perhaps the most dreaded provisions of the Bankruptcy Code relate to cramdown; that is, the right of the court to confirm a plan of reorganization over the objection of a class of creditors, provided at least one class affirms the plan and the court finds the plan to be "fair and equitable." Special provisions with respect to secured creditors, particularly holders of nonrecourse mortgages, permit the nonrecourse lender to elect one of two options in a cramdown situation. It can convert its mortgage to a recourse mortgage by retaining a secured claim only to the extent of the value of the property, with any deficiency being converted to an unsecured claim. Or it can elect to remain nonrecourse and have the full amount of its claim secured regardless of the value of the collateral. In either case a valuation proceeding will be necessary and since most parties like to avoid such proceedings for fear of the outcome (not to mention the time and expense involved), there is significant inducement for a negotiated settlement.

Assuming a settlement is not reached and the lender has a $5 million loan balance secured by a property valued at $4 million, under the first option, the lender would have a secured claim against the property for $4 million and an unsecured claim for $1 million. Under the second option, the amount of the secured claim would be $5 million but there would be no unsecured claim. For a cramdown against the lender to be "fair and equitable," the plan must provide that the lender receive deferred cash payments in the amount of its secured claim having a present value at least equal to the value of the collateral. Consequently, under either option, the lender would be receiving deferred payments having a present value of $4 million although the deferred cash payments under option 1 would total $4 million and under option 2 would total $5 million. In the latter case, the actual value would be reduced by reducing the interest rate or extending the term or a combination of both.

In the foregoing situation, the advantage to the lender holding the secured and unsecured claims would be that the value of the unsecured claim would be grouped with the class of unsecured creditors possibly enabling the lender to control this class and defeat the cramdown. In addition, if there are other assets of the debtor to be realized upon, the unsecured claim may have some value.

The lender would be advised to opt for a fully secured claim in circumstances where little would be realized on the unsecured claim, refinancing or foreclosure in the future seems likely, the amount of the unsecured claim to the lender would not be significant in relation to other unsecured creditors, where a write-down of the investment is not desired or where the property is being sold. The chief advantage to the lender in having a fully secured claim is that if there is a subsequent default under the plan of reorganization, the secured creditor would get the benefit of the appreciation rather than the debtor.

It should be noted that the findings of valuation for the purpose of automatic stay and adequate protection are not binding for the purpose of the plan of reorganization or cramdown. Nonetheless, judges are only human and if the hearings are close enough in time, the evidence from one hearing is bound to be applied in the other. This presents the lender with a dilemma since it is to the lender's advantage to assign a lower value to the property for adequate protection purposes and a higher value for cramdown purposes. However, if the lender comes in with a very low value at the beginning of the case and loses, it may be prejudicing its case later on. Consequently, before the lender takes a position on value, it must take a prospective view of the entire proceedings and not just look at the initial stages.

Preferences and Fraudulent Transfers

The law of preferences and fraudulent transfers is often referred to as the "strong arm clause" of the Bankruptcy Code since it grants creditors of an estate certain voiding powers in order to provide for "a fair and equitable distribution of assets among creditors."

A transfer under the Code is defined very broadly and includes any disposition of any interest; for example, a transfer of possession custody or control with or without transfer of title. Any such transfer will be deemed preferential and can be voided if it is "(i) To or for the benefit of a creditor, (ii) for or on account of an antecendent debt, (iii) while the debtor was insolvent, (iv) within 90 days (one year in the case of insiders) before the filing of a petition in bankruptcy and (v) the transfer enables the creditor to receive more than it would have received if the transfer had not been made and there had been liquidation." Consequently, most transfers within 90 days of the filing of a bankruptcy petition will be considered preferential. Of course, this can have a profound effect upon a workout situation when one of the factors in the problem loan is the borrower's financial situation. Because of the preference problem, lenders must take particular care before finalizing any workouts so as not to run the risk of having the transaction voided should the borrower subsequently file in bankruptcy.

If a transfer is deemed actually or constructively fraudulent (the existence of an actual creditor who was defrauded is not necessary) within one year of the filing of a bankruptcy petition, it may also be voided. For actual fraud, it must be shown that there was *actual intent to hinder, delay or defraud* creditors, existing or future, real or imagined. Value is not material. Although this is a subjective, factual question, there are certain situations which by their very nature are deemed "badges of fraud"; for example, where the property is conveyed during the pendency of an action against the debtor or shortly before the filing of a petition, particularly when the debtor maintains control of the property, or if the transfer is secret and/or transfers all of the debtor's property.

To establish that there was constructive fraud, it must be shown basically that the transfer was made for less than fair market value *and* that the debtor was or became insolvent at the time or as a result of the transfer.

Recent Court Decisions

Recent court decisions interpreting the law of fraudulent transfers have had a profound and disturbing effect upon the lending community. In *Durrett* v. *Washington National Insurance Company,* 21 F. 2d201 5th Cir., (Tex. 1980), followed by *Abramson* v. *Lakewood Bank & Trust Co.,* 647 F. 2d 547 5th Cir. (Tex. 1981), the court held that a nonjudicial foreclosure sale within one year prior to the filing of a bankruptcy petition was subject to being set aside as fraudulent if the purchaser did not pay reasonably equivalent value (i.e., approximately 70% of the worth of the property) for the property at the time of sale. The rationale of the court was that the foreclosure sale constituted a transfer within the meaning of the Bankruptcy Code. A Nevada bankruptcy court followed this line of reasoning in the case of In re Madrid, 10 B.R. 795 v.s. Bankruptcy Court (D. Nev., May 1981), but the Bankruptcy Appellate Panel for the 9th Circuit reversed the decision (BAP No. NV-81-1106-HVE, Bankruptcy No. 81-00038 [BAP, 9th Cir. June 22, 1982]), holding that the purchase price at the foreclosure sale, properly conducted without fraud or collusion, was deemed to be made for reasonably equivalent value within the meaning of the code.

These cases are contrasted with the case of In re Alsop, 14 B.R. 982 (D. Alaska 1981), wherein the bankruptcy court, after considering the Durrett, Lakewood Bank and In re Madrid cases, held that the transfer took place when the mortgage was perfected and not at the subsequent foreclosure sale. This case brings a glimmer of hope to the lending community; however, until the issue is finally resolved by the United States Supreme Court or by Congress, (legislation in this regard has already been introduced in S. 445 by Senator Robert Dole [R-Kansas]), uncertainty in this area will continue to abound.

The recent Supreme Court Decision overturning portions of the Bankruptcy Code due to the status of the bankruptcy judges does not seem to have had any significant effect upon the lending community. Until this matter is resolved, most lenders faced with bankruptcy situations are simply requiring that the district court approve all actions taken by the bankruptcy court that may be subject to possible voidance. Most district courts have been cooperative in this regard, resulting in minimal delays for approval of plans of reorganization and the like.

A CASE STUDY: THE WORKOUT OF A PROBLEM LOAN

This section sets forth the case study of a fictitious workout consisting of a combination of facts, real and imagined, that occurred in several transactions in which the author participated:

WORKING OUT A PROBLEM LOAN*

In Spring 1979, Patient National Trust Co. made a construction loan to Busy Bee Borrower for the construction of an office building in a growing area that was somewhat removed from the lender's home base. Before making any advances on its loan, the construction lender assured itself that the permanent loan commitment was in full force and effect and that all the leases required by the permanent commitment were executed and in form satisfactory to the permanent lender. The borrower complied with all the usual preconstruction requirements, and the construction loan closed on schedule.

The Development Sours. For about one year, actual construction progressed on a timely basis with no apparent problems. Then the foundation began to collapse. Not the foundation of the building, but the basis of the loan. Tenant interest in the project was based on the anticipated construction of a major regional development project. Work on that project ceased as the result of an extended workers' strike, and the ripple effect of that dislocation was felt throughout the area. The tenants that had wanted space in the partially completed office building no longer desired to occupy their premises. Miraculously, ironclad leases turned out to be so porous that they were hardly worth the paper they were written on. At the same time, the borrower had so overextended his resources on other development projects that he was teetering on the brink of bankruptcy. Consequently, the general contractor and subcontractors who had been working on the office building were rapidly losing confidence in the developer's ability to meet his obligations. To make matters even worse, sky-high interest rates had depleted the project's interest reserves and the borrower ran out of funds to pay the remaining interest due on the loan.

The construction lender realized that its collateral for the loan now consisted of a partially completed building with no preleasing, an insolvent borrower, a depleted interest reserve, and an all but officially terminated take-out commitment. It was time for the lender to make some hard choices. Its first and most obvious problem was whether or

---

*This section, written by the author, is reprinted by permission from the *Real Estate Review*, Vol. 11, No. 3, Fall 1981, Copyright © 1981, Warren, Gorham and Lamont, Inc., 210 South Street, Boston, Mass. All rights reserved.

not to declare a default under the terms of the loan and institute foreclosure proceedings.

There were a number of arguments against foreclosure. The borrower declared his intention to fight any foreclosure proceedings by declaring bankruptcy. The general contractor took the understandable position that unless he were paid, his men would walk off the job, and he would bring them back only under a new contract that presumably contained higher costs. The remote location of the premises was also a factor that the lender had to consider. Did it really want to own this distant partially completed project? The lender's alternative was to reach some kind of workout arrangement with the borrower.

The Lender Decides not to Foreclose. The lender's prime concern was to complete the building as soon as possible and at the lowest practical cost. This made foreclosure an unacceptable alternative at this stage of the workout. Once the building was completed, the lender would not continue to be subject to ever-rising construction costs.

In order to keep the project going, the lender took a calculated risk and used the funds that, in accordance with the terms of the loan, had been set aside as a reserve for tenant finish work, to substitute for the depleted interest reserve. Actually, this was hardly a great risk. The funds in the tenant finish reserve had been set aside to assure the lender that when the building was finished, the developer would have funds to proceed with the activities that would be required to lease up the building. But there would be no funds to complete the building unless funds from the reserve for tenant finish were used to refurbish the interest reserve.

Four months later the building was completed. The loan proceeds were totally depleted and the permanent lender had officially terminated its commitment. No portion of the new structure had been preleased. And, the borrower remained insolvent. The sole bright spot was the fact that the strike that had stalled the major regional development project had ended and the workers and feeder industries were slowly coming back to the area. This promised substantial rewards to the owner of the newly completed office building, if he could produce the office space for which demand was reviving. It was time for the lender to "lay down the law" to the borrower.

A Further Compromise. A meeting was scheduled at the lender's office attended by the borrower and several of the lender's personnel. As a preliminary, the lender's representatives asked the borrower to come up with the funds to pay off the construction loan. The borrower replied that this was impossible. He had no funds of his own, and there was just no permanent financing available, especially on projects with no preleasing.

Would the borrower deed the property to the lender in lieu of foreclosure? "Not without a fight," responded the borrower flatly. He assured the lender that any foreclosure action would delay the recruiting of tenants and prevent the lender from having the first crack at the companies that were once again moving into the area.

The lender's representatives huddled together and engaged in a violent debate. They were about equally divided between those who favored foreclosure and those who wanted to arrange a workout. Those favoring the institution of immediate foreclosure proceedings reasoned that since the office building was the borrower's sole asset, the borrower's delaying tactics would only hold up a foreclosure sale by at most six months, even if the borrower did file in bankruptcy. The others, who may have suffered through protracted foreclosure negotiations in the past, expressed skepticism about the optimistic time assumptions. They advocated that the lender offer the borrower some form of consideration in exchange for his voluntary conveyance of the property. They didn't want to lose out on the opportunity of obtaining choice tenants in the present leasing environment.

The compromise won out. A negotiating stance was then taken, and the meeting, with all parties once again in attendance, resumed. The borrower had, the lender's representatives told him, the following three options:

- He could deed the property to the lender and receive a percentage of any gain that the lender derived if and when it subsequently sold the property.
- He could arrange to sell the property to a third party acceptable to lender, whereupon the lender would recast its loan into a five-year interim loan in favor of the third party.
- If he completed neither of these courses of action during the next twenty days, the lender would institute foreclosure proceedings,

and the borrower would lose the property through a foreclosure sale.

Needless to say, the borrower refused to consider the third choice and reiterated that he would vigorously fight foreclosure. He expressed significant interest in the second choice, but he expressed doubts that he could find a purchaser within the twenty days. Reluctantly, he agreed, after considerable negotiation about the percentage of consideration that he would receive in the event of a sale, that, if he could not find a buyer within twenty days, he would deed the property to the lender.

Fortunately, the property was well constructed and marketable. Because several parties had expressed interest in the property during the first year of construction, there was even a list of prospective buyers who already had knowledge of the property, were financially solvent, who were acceptable to the lender, and who, if necessary, could act in a relatively short time.

The Borrower Finds a Buyer. At the end of the twenty-day period the borrower reported that he had reached tentative agreement with a potential buyer who met the lender's requirements for financial responsibility. However, he needed additional time to negotiate the sale. The lender satisfied itself that a deal was in fact in the making and agreed to assist the borrower in selling the property by working with the prospective purchaser. It agreed further to give the negotiating parties a reasonable amount of time in which to iron out the details of the transaction.

Weeks passed, and although all parties appeared to be negotiating in good faith, nothing was accomplished. The lender, torn between the possible loss of a potential purchaser and the prospect of endless negotiations, gave the borrower another deadline. It established a specific date by which time the borrower had to implement one of the original three choices. It called a meeting for the deadline date at the office of its local counsel.

A Deed in Lieu of Foreclosure. The meeting took place on schedule. However, the details of the sale to the third party had still not been made final. The borrower continued to insist that they were very close, and he requested another extension.

To this the lender replied flatly, "No!" The lender insisted on enforcing one of three options. But it compromised mildly. It took the deed to the property from the borrower and promised the borrower a certain amount of time in which to broker a transaction between the lender and the prospective purchaser. The lender further agreed not to sell the property, without the borrower's consent, to the prospective purchaser for a period of one year from the date of the deed.

For the first time the lender felt in complete control of the circumstances. The prospective purchaser, who had previously been convinced that the lender and borrower had their backs against the wall, was now faced with a deadline by which time he either had to buy the property or take himself out of the bidding. Since he had already invested a considerable amount of time, effort and money in the potential transaction, doing appraisal and preliminary syndication work, he really did want to close on the purchase. Foot dragging became jogging, and near the end of the deadline, jogging became a race to complete the sale prior to the cut-off date.

Negotiations over the terms of the mortgage that the lender would give the prospective purchaser commenced almost immediately after the borrower deeded the property to the lender. When these negotiations also hit a snag, all the concerned parties met once again at the office of lender's counsel in a final attempt to resolve their differences. The borrower and prospective purchaser had agreed quite early on the consideration to be paid the borrower for the sale. So the lender and the purchaser were now haggling about the terms of the interim mortgage and the costs involved in bringing the construction loan current. The prospective purchaser pushed the lender to accommodate his "tax considerations" and the lender traded these off for fees and charges attached to the loan.

The Sale is Concluded.   It is always difficult to deal from weakness. Perhaps the prospective purchaser could not rid itself of the belief that the lender was desperate for a deal. Perhaps the lender had compromised so often before that the purchaser felt that there would always be one more compromise. For, after a full day of haggling, when the lender's personnel finally raised their hands in resignation and stated,

"This is it, take it or leave it," the prospective purchaser still insisted that the lender grant further concessions and that if the lender ceased negotiations, it would sue for damages. The borrower then became frantic. His deed to the property was in the lender's hands. If the sale fell through, even his brokerage commission would be lost. He too threatened to sue the lender if it could not come to agreement with the prospective purchaser.

The lender's personnel realized that neither party had any real grounds for a lawsuit. The time for compromise was over. They adjourned the meeting until the next day, telling the others that at that time the deal would either be concluded or abandoned.

The next morning the parties got together and consummated the sale in one hour. The purchaser had been persuaded that as usual the "man with the money" was in the driver's seat rather than behind the eightball. All parties received substantially what they bargained for and seemed genuinely satisfied with their respective positions.

There are several morals to be found in this case history of a workout of a problem loan. The first moral is that patience is a virtue. The lender is not always wise to rush into foreclosure proceedings if, by working with the borrower and/or third parties, it can make arrangements to resolve a loan's problems.

The second moral is that there usually comes a time when the accommodating lender must say, "That's enough! I have compromised as much as I can. I now insist on my rights."

There are two morals suggested at the end of the article. They deal with accommodation and assertion of rights. If you combine the two, you would come up with a single truism to be followed by lenders in all workout situations: "It's best to compromise, except when it's better to be tough." The key is to know which alternative to choose.

11
The Pay-Off

Borrowers are usually quite anxious to complete the project and have the construction loan repaid. In most cases, there is considerable incentive for them to do this since they will likely be looking forward to closing a permanent long-term mortgage or an interim mortgage at a significantly lower interest rate or pocketing the profits of an arranged sale of the property. In either situation, the borrower will be exerting considerable pressure on all parties concerned to close the new transaction and satisfy the old one, that is, the construction loan.

NOTICE

When the borrower is nearing readiness to repay the construction loan (this will usually entail completion of construction and compliance with all the provisions of the take-out commitment), it should notify the construction lender several weeks in advance of the proposed payoff date and request payoff figures, instructions where to send funds to the construction lender and release documents or assignments to the take-out lender of the construction loan note and mortgage among other documents. This notice may be by mail or by telephone and is usually directed to the lender's attorney, the loan correspondent or servicing agent or the loan administrator, depending upon who the borrower has had the most contact with. However, regardless of to whom the notice is sent, ultimately it will be the responsibility of the loan administrator to respond to the borrower's requests and otherwise coordinate the last remaining facets of the loan.

ROLE OF THE LOAN ADMINISTRATOR

Checking Records

The first step of the loan administrator upon receipt of the notice from the borrower should be to check his records to ascertain whether the loan was scheduled to be paid off at this time. If the loan has several months remaining and an early prepayment was not anticipated, the lender's cash projections could be severely impacted by the repayment and the loan underwriters should be alerted. In many instances, the borrower's action may emanate from its ability to obtain less expensive construction money or interim financing elsewhere. If this is the case, the lender may be willing to reduce its interest rate in order to keep a well-secured and profitable loan on its books. Negotiations on this as well as other matters, if desired, should commence as soon as possible after the lender becomes aware of the borrower's intent to pay off its loan.

Notify Attorney

In addition to alerting the loan underwriters, the loan administrator should also request the lender's attorney to review the loan documents to see if the borrower has the right to repay the construction loan. The answer to this legal question will obviously have a significant bearing on the lender's negotiating position. In fact, in situations where prepayment of the loan is prohibited, lenders have often exacted a fee from the borrower for permitting the early payoff. The amount of the fee will usually be roughly equivalent to the lender's loss of bargain; that is, the profitability of the loan to the lender over its remaining term.

Contact Borrower

All of the foregoing assumes that the borrower is ready, willing and able to pay off the construction loan and has so notified the lender. What happens if the lender never hears from the borrower concerning repayment? The answer is that the loan administrator must contact the borrower and remind him that arrangements need to be made to satisfy the construction loan. The periodic status reports on each loan prepared by the loan administrator should alert him to the approaching maturity date of the loan and trigger his call to the borrower. This contact should take place at least six weeks before the maturity date, assuming there are no problems concerning the loan which would precipitate earlier action.

The reasons why the borrower may not take the initiative in arranging for the satisfaction of the construction loan are varied. The most common reason (assuming construction is completed and the loan is current) is that the borrower just does not have the necessary funds to repay the loan. Either the provider of take-out financing has delayed its closing or the borrower never obtained a take-out commitment and does not have sufficient funds out-of-pocket. In these instances, the borrower will most likely request an extension of the loan in order to provide it with more time to arrange for permanent financing or a sale of the property. Depending on the borrower's financial conditions and whether the need for a workout exists (see chapter 10), the lender will usually grant a reasonable extension of the loan provided the loan is current and its position is not otherwise impaired. The lender's prime objective at this point is to get its loan repaid. Thus, depending upon the circumstances (e.g., the ability of the borrower to pay and the value of the property in relation to the debt), the lender may not exact any consideration for extending the loan either in the form of an extension fee or by increasing the interest rate during the extended period.

Compile Pay-off Figures

Regardless of whether the borrower notifies the lender of its intent to pay off the loan or whether the pay-off comes after the loan is extended, several days prior to the repayment date the loan administrator should contact the lender's accounting department and receive figures setting forth the outstanding principal balance of the loan, all unpaid and accrued interest to the anticipated pay-off date, the per diem rate of interest in case the loan is not repaid exactly on schedule and any other sums that may be due from the borrower under the loan. These figures should then be furnished the borrower and the escrow agent, if any, handling the closing of the take-out financing. The escrow agent should also receive satisfaction documents or assignments to the permanent lender, as the case may be, of the construction loan documentation with instructions that these documents are not to be released unless and until the construction loan has been repaid in full. If this has not taken place by a certain date, the documents should be returned to the lender.

Confirmation

To confirm the actual amount needed to repay the construction loan, the instruction letter should call for the escrow agent (or borrower if there is no escrow agent) to contact the loan administrator on the repayment date to verify the interest figures. This is necessary since most construction loans call for interest at a floating rate tied either to a specific bank's designated prime rate or to the weekly average commercial paper rate.

The importance of requiring last-minute confirmation of the amount needed to satisfy the construction loan and otherwise carefully drafting the instruction letter cannot be overemphasized. For should insufficient funds be forwarded to the lender, there will always be recourse against the escrow agent, among others, to recover these funds. This is particularly relevant where the construction lender has sent to the escrow agent the satisfaction or assignment documents and these documents have been released, discharging the construction lender's lien against the property. Of course, in most instances recourse can also be had against the borrower; however, lenders at this point would much rather be dealing with a solvent escrow agent (oftentimes a reputable title company) to recover the sums still due them rather than a borrower who has closed its take-out commitment and thinks the construction loan is past history. Recovery of outstanding funds becomes a much easier task where the lender still retains the construction loan documents and has not released or assigned them to any other party. The lender just refuses to discharge its lien until it has been paid in full.

PROCESSING FEE

Sometimes lenders will charge the borrower a fee for processing the release or assignment documents and accumulating the necessary information to enable the borrower to repay the construction loan. Payment of this fee, which is usually nominal is almost always mandatory when residential mortgages are paid off; however, it is not universally charged with regard to commercial mortgages. In fact, since a few states have statutory provision requiring the lender to provide a satisfaction form (e.g., Florida), national lenders would be well advised to inquire of their local counsel in the states where they do business whether such fees may be charged at all.

ASSIGNMENT TO PERMANENT MORTGAGEE

When an assignment of the construction loan documents to the permanent mortgagee is involved, arrangements should be made well in advance of the permanent loan closing between the respective attorneys for the construction lender and permanent lender. The form of the assignment documents should be agreed upon as well as any estoppel statement regarding the loan required by the permanent lender. In this regard, it is customary for the permanent lender to seek certification from the construction lender as to the existing principal balance of the loan, that there are no defaults under the loan or defenses to payment (or right of setoff) and that the construction lender has the good and lawful right to assign the construction loan documents free and clear of any liens whatsoever. This is not to say that such certifications will always be granted. In particular, construction lenders typically limit certifications regarding defaults and defenses "to the best of their knowledge," and although generally they certify that they have the right to assign the loan documents, they will not warrant them against liens. This is more properly the role of the title insurer. In addition, the construction lender must take care to assign the note "without recourse" to preclude the permanent lender from going after it should the borrower subsequently default in payments of loan installments.

RECEIPT OF FUNDS

After all of the foregoing has been said and done, the role of the loan administrator is still not over. For arrangements need to be made with the lender's cashier's or treasurer's department to coordinate the actual receipt of money by the lender. In this regard, the treasurer should be advised as far in advance as is possible, of the date the loan proceeds are expected to be repaid. The treasurer will then attempt to match these incoming funds with obligations that the lender itself has to pay. Oftentimes, the lender will use the incoming funds before they actually arrive provided it is reasonably assured that they are on their way and will in fact be deposited in the lender's account by the end of the day. In this regard, lenders should insist that any funds due it be sent by federal reserve wire transfer rather than paid by check. In this manner, lenders will have immediate use of the funds wired rather than having to wait until the borrower's check (which in all instances should be either a certified or official bank check) clears. Once the funds have actually arrived in the construction lender's account, the loan administrator can then say "Amen" and his role has finally ended.

Index

Access, 121
Accounting. *See* Construction loan accounting
Air rights, 37, 121
ALTA. *See* American Land Title Association
Alterations and additions, 11-13
American Land Title Association, 121. *See also* Title insurance companies
Apartment projects. *See* Residential properties
Application. *See* Loan application
Application and certificate for payment, 98, 171
   forms of, 108-115, 118
Appraisals, 6, 22, 69, 96
   capitalization rate, 25
Architects/Engineers, 22, 26, 30-33, 96-97, 152, 186
   form of architect of record certification, 102
   role in loan underwriting process, 30-33
      review of costs, 31-32
      review of plans and specifications, 32
Articles of incorporation, 92
Assignment of lessor's interest in leases, 87. *See also* Leases
Assignment of rents. *See* Assignment of lessor's interest in leases
Attorneys, 22, 37. *See also* Borrower's counsel, Lender's attorney and Permanent lender's attorney
Attorneys' fees. *See* Fees and charges

Balancing, 72, 74, 98, 162, 173
Bankruptcy, 187, 189, 193-198
   automatic stays, 194-195
   bankruptcy code, 189, 194-196
      strong arm clause, 196
   cramdowns, 195-196
   effect upon foreclosure sale, 197-198
   preferences and fraudulent transfers, 196-197
Banks, 2, 3, 7, 27, 55
   as sources of financing, 7
   as sponsors of REITs, 2, 3
Bonding companies, 183, 190, 191
Bonds, 8-9, 40, 71, 97-98, 137, 164, 185
   as protection against mechanics liens, 98, 137
   bonding of general contractor, 6
   completion bonds, 185
   industrial development bonds, 8-9
   lender as dual obligee, 97, 137
   payment and performance bonds, 40, 71, 97-98, 185
Borings and soil reports, 96-97
Borrowers, 24, 37-39, 54, 90, 161, 186. *See also* Developers
   affidavit, 90
   defaults by, 54
   defenses to lenders' rights, 186
   equity requirements, 38-39
   interest in the property, 37
   nature of borrowing entity, 37
   statement as to source of construction funds, 97
      form of, 117
   view of buy-sell or tripartite agreement, 161
Borrower's counsel, 86, 90-94
   documents to be submitted by, 91-93
      checklist of, 94
   opinion of, 90

Boston, Massachusetts, 13
Brokers, 2, 23
Budget, 163, 164, 183, 184
Builders, 186. *See also* Borrowers and Developers
Builders risk casualty insurance. *See* Hazard insurance
Building code, 32, 186
Building loan agreement, 67, 68, 87, 88, 91
  effect of changes on problem loan, 192
  schedule of soft cost items, 42
Building permit, 23, 27, 34, 92–93, 185
Bullet loans, 150. *See also* Permanent take-out commitment
Business requirements for closing, 93–100
  checklist of, 94–95
Buy-sell/tripartite agreement, 26, 86, 89–90, 155–156, 157–161, 192
  borrower's view, 161
  construction lender's view, 158–159
  permanent lender's view, 159–160

California, 4, 14, 49–50, 131
Capitalization rate, 25. *See also* Appraisals
Casualty insurance. *See* Hazard insurance
Certificate for payment. *See* Application and certificate for payment
Certificate of deposit, 25, 154
Certificate of occupancy, 27, 152, 176
Change orders, 44
Chicago, Illinois, 10, 14
Client relationships, 49
Closing report, 167–168
  form of, 169
Commercial banks. *See* Banks
Commercial construction, 9–16. *See also* Nonresidential construction
  during 1983, 9
  during 1984, 10–16
    by type of construction, 10–12, 14
    by region, 12–13
    by top ten states, 15
    by cities, 15–16
Commitment for permanent financing. *See* Permanent take-out commitment
Commitment for title insurance. *See* Title insurance
Completion bonds. *See* Bonds
Completion date, 184

Condemnation proceeds, 86, 88, 91
  application toward restoration of premises, 86, 91
Condominiums. *See* Residential properties
Congress, 17
Construction contracts, 22, 40, 43, 70, 163–164, 192
  assignment of, 88–89
  consent to assignment and undertakings to perform, 89
  effect of modification during workout, 192
  major subcontracts, 40
  retainage provisions, 45
  to which lender is not a party, 43
Construction financing, 7
  sources of, 7
Construction loan accounting, 177–181, 190
  calculation of interest, 178–179
  effect of foreclosure, 190
  providing pay-off figures, 207
Construction loan agreement. *See* Building loan agreement
Construction loan commitment, 50. *See* generally Chapter 5
  amendment process, 74–77
  "bare essentials" commitments, 66–67
  "detailed" commitments, 67–68
  in participations, 50
  moderately detailed commitments, 68
  sample "detailed" commitment, 68–74
    form of, 78–84
  special conditions, 74
Construction loan escrow, 174–175. *See also* Title insurance companies
Construction risks, 182
Consumer credit protection, 128
Contiguity, 122
Contracts. *See* Construction contracts
Correspondents, 23
Costs, 22, 26–27, 31–32, 37–38, 42, 69, 167, 188, 191, 193
  cost estimates, 22, 31–32
  cost overruns, 167, 188, 191
  detailed cost breakdown, 26, 69, 97
    in form of application for payment, 108–115
  hard costs, 31, 38
  land acquisition costs, 37

nonqualified costs, 38, 39, 42
preliminary cost breakdown, 23
replacement costs, 193
soft costs, 31, 37, 38
Covenants, conditions and restrictions, 121–122
Creditors, 194–196. *See also* Bankruptcy
liens of, 124–125
Cross-defaults, 41
Curtesy, 123. *See also* Dower

Dallas, Texas, 10, 14
Debt service, 24, 25
escrow, 153–4
of long-term mortgage, 24, 25
Deed of Trust. *See* Mortgages
Deeds, 122
in lieu of foreclosure, 188–189
Defaults, 43, 45. *See also* Foreclosure
by borrower, 43, 45
in contracts, 43
in leases, 45
related participation agreement provisions, 54, 55
cross-defaults, 41
Deficiency judgment, 187. *See also* Foreclosure
Denver, Colorado, 10, 12
Developers, 23. *See also* Borrowers and Builders
Disbursement agreement, 88
Disbursement methods, 52–53, 170–171
in participations, 52–53
progress payments, 171
prerequisites to, 171–172
voucher plan, 170
District of Columbia. *See* Washington, D.C.
"Doing business" requirements, 33, 186–187, 189
Dower, 123. *See also* Curtesy
Draw requests, 52, 98, 183. *See also* Disbursement methods in form of application and certificate for payment, 118

Easements, 41, 91, 121, 122
light and air easements, 121
navigational easements, 121

Ecological laws, 91. *See also* Environmental requirements
Economic Tax Recovery Act of 1981 (ERTA), 12. *See also* Taxes
Election of remedies, 189
Elevator maintenance contracts, 155. *See also* Construction contracts
Encroachments and projections, 122–123
retractive encroachments, 123
Energy, 18, 19, 34
costs, 19
related industries, 18
requirements, 34
Engineers, 97. *See also* Architects/Engineers
certification of engineer of record, 97
form of, 105
engineered fill certification, 97
form of, 106
Environmental requirements, 32, 34, 40, 152, 186. *See also* Energy
Equity capital, 38–39, 188, 191
Equity purchaser, 149–150, 161
Escrow agent, 175, 207. *See also* Title insurance companies
construction loan escrow, 174–175
Estoppel statement, 209

Fast track construction, 27, 76, 96, 163
Feasibility study, 6, 24, 186
in workouts, 186
Federal Housing Administration (FHA), 40
Federal Reserve Bank, 17. *See also* Interest rates
Federal securities acts, 53
Fees and charges, 72, 155, 181, 193, 207–209. *See also* Costs
accountants' fees, 193
as interests, 181
attorneys' fees, 72, 193
extension fees, 207
processing fee, 208–209
required by permanent lender, 155
Fee simple title, 37, 120. *See also* Title
Financial statements, 23–24, 28–30
as reflection of net worth, 28
balance sheet, 29
income statement, 29–30
pro forma income and expense statement, 23–24

214 INDEX

Floor funding, 39. *See also* Permanent take-out commitment
Florida, 4, 13, 14, 20, 77, 209
Force majeure, 164
Foreclosure, 46, 187–189
   effect of bankruptcy upon foreclosure sale, 197–198
   of ground leases, 46
   redemption rights, 190
Foreign capital, 8
Foundation completion certification, 97, 153
   form of, 107
Foundation permit, 17, 76. *See also* Fast track construction

Gap financing, 38, 191. *See also* Permanent take-out commitment
General contract, 38, 39–40, 192. *See also* Construction contracts
General contractor, 96, 132–133, 137, 185, 188, 192. *See also* Subcontractors
   as mechanic's lien claimant, 132–133
   bonding of, 6, 137
Georgia, 20
Gores. *See* Strips and gores
Government approvals, 34, 40, 69, 152. *See also* Environmental requirements
Ground lease. *See* Leases
Guarantees, 6, 40, 75, 155
   in form of master lease, 155
   of completion and repayment, 87
   release as consideration for deed in lieu, 189
   required by permanent take-out commitment, 154–155
Guarantors, 23, 24, 183, 187, 190–192
   general partners as, 75

Hard costs. *See* Costs
Hazard insurance, 88, 97, 192
   application of proceeds, 86, 91
Holdbacks, 38. *See also* Retainage
Hospitality facilities, 11, 13, 48
Hotels. *See* Hospitality facilities
Houston, Texas, 10, 12

Illinois, 14, 20, 135
Industrial development bonds (IDB's), 8, 9
Industrial space, 10, 12

Inflation, 4, 17, 24, 193
Ingress and egress. *See* Access
Inspecting architect, 69, 96, 97, 163, 165–167, 176. *See also* Architect/Engineer
   agreement, form of, 104
   cost certification, form of, 116
   role during loan administration, 165–167
   scope of services, form letter outlining, 103
Insurance. *See* specifically Hazard insurance and Title insurance
Interest, 72. *See also* Costs and Usury
   fees as interest, 181
   interest reserves, 3, 86, 164
   methods of calculating, 178–179
Interest rates, 17, 177, 184
   prime rate, 3
Internal Revenue Code, 1. *See also* Taxes
Iowa, 20

Joint venture, 149. *See also* Permanent take-out commitment agreement, 92
Judgment liens, 124

Kansas, 20
Kentucky, 19

Land purchase leasebacks, 7, 149. *See also* Permanent take-out commitment
Land trust agreement, 92
Lawyers Title Insurance Company of Richmond Virginia, 138. *See also* Title insurance companies
Lead lender. *See* Loan participations
Leasehold loans, 45–56, 124. *See also* Leases
Leases, 24, 34–35, 45–56, 124. *See also* Leases
Leases, 24, 34–35, 45–46, 71, 123, 153, 185
   ground leases, 37, 124
   letters of intent, 23
   long-term net lease, 24, 45–46
   major tenant lease, 153, 185
   master lease, 155
   preleasing, 24, 35
   short-term lease, 24
   subordination to mortgage, 123
   tenant finish work, 32, 153
Leasing agents, 24

INDEX

Lenders attorney, 85–86, 93, 167–168, 183, 185–186, 205, 206. *See also* Attorneys
  loan documents prepared by, 86–91
    check list of, 93–94
  preparation of closing report, 167–168
    form of closing report, 169
  role during loan administration, 167–168
  verification of zoning, 93
Lending limitations, 48
Lending policy, 22–23
Letter of assurances, 90, 91, 156, 161
Letter of credit, 25, 38, 40, 71, 98–99, 153, 166, 191
  form of, 119
Liens. *See* specific headings
Lien waivers, 135, 173, 192. *See also* Mechanics liens
Life insurance companies, 2, 3, 8, 69
  as sponsors of REITs, 2, 3
Lis pendens, 125
Loan administration. *See* generally Chapter 9
Loan administrator, 22, 95–99, 182–183, 205–210
  insuring compliance with business items, 95–99
  role at time loan is paid-off, 206–210
Loan amount, 73
Loan application, 23
Loan documents, 93–94, 193. *See also* specific headings
  alleged defects in, 186
  changes necessitated by workout, 193
  checklist of, 93–94
Loan officer. *See* Loan underwriter
Loan participations. *See* generally Chapter 4
Loan servicing, 48, 50, 53
Loan underwriter, 22, 26, 85, 93, 187, 206
Long-term financing, 7–8. *See also* Permanent take-out commitment
  sources of, 7–8
Los Angeles, California, 12
Loss reserves, 190

Major subcontractors. *See* Subcontractors
Management agreement, 90
Marshalling of assets, 189
Maryland, 131

Master lease. *See* Leases
Materialmen. *See* Subcontractors
Materials, 73–74, 88, 166. *See also* Uniform Commercial Code (UCC) Financing Statements
  stored on-site, 73–74
Maturity date, 72
Mechanics' liens, 41, 42–43, 98, 131–147, 173–175, 183, 185–189, 191
  notice of claim, 185
  priority to construction lender, 135–136
  priority to mechanic's lienor, 135
  state survey of mechanics' lien laws, 140–147
  the "New York" system, 132
  the "Pennsylvania" system, 132–133
  title insurance protection, 70, 124–125, 129–130, 136–137, 174–175, 185
    construction loan escrow, 174
    pending disbursements clause, 125
Michigan, 20
Mineral reservations, 127. *See also* Subsurface rights
Minnesota, 20
Missouri, 20
Mortgage bankers, 2, 8, 24
  as sponsors of REITs, 2
Mortgagee in possession, 188. *See also* Foreclosure
Mortgage/equity combinations, 7, 149. *See also* Permanent take-out commitment
Mortgage liens, 124
Mortgage loan underwriter. *See* Loan underwriter
Mortgages 40, 86–87, 148, 150
  additional interest provision mortgages, 7, 148
  conventional mortgage, 150
  interest rate adjusted mortgages, 7, 148
  interim mortgage, 205
  junior mortgage, 188, 189
  nonrecourse mortgage, 195
  permanent long-term mortgage, 151, 205, 209
  priority versus mechanics liens, 131–136
  with partnership interest, 7, 149
Motels. *See* Hospitality facilities

Navigational servitudes, 125–126
Nebraska, 20

Negative pledge agreement, 40
New England, 13, 20
New Jersey, 20
New Mexico, 19
New York Board of Title Underwriters (NYBTU), 121
New York City, 13
New York State, 14, 20, 41, 135, 173, 195
Nonresidential construction, 4–6, 9–16
   by census regions
      1977–82, 5
      1980–82, 10
   by cities, 1982–84, 15, 16
   by regions, 1982–84, 15
   by states,
      1977–82, 4–5
      1982–84, 15
   by type of building, 1982–84, 14
   components of, 9
Note. See Promissory note
Notices, 95, 185, 205
   of business requirements for closing, 95
   form of, 100
   of intent to pay-off construction loan, 205
   of mechanic's lien claim, 185
Nursing homes, 18

Oil and gas reservations, 127. See also Subsurface rights
Ohio, 20
Office buildings, 10, 12, 36
   inflation, effect upon, 17
   inner city, 36
Opinion of borrower's counsel, 90–91. See also Borrower's counsel
OSHA, 32

Parking requirements, 32, 93
   parking garage, 37
Participants. See Loan participations
Participation agreement, 51–56. See also Loan participations
   form of, 56–64
Participation certificate, 51. See also Loan participations
   form of, 65
Partnership, 75, 149
   agreement, 76, 92
   as borrowing entity, 75

Payment and performance bonds. See Bonds
Pennsylvania, 20, 131
Pension funds, 8
Performance bonds. See Bonds
Permanent commitment. See Permanent take-out commitment
Permanent financing, 38, 39. See also Permanent take-out commitment
Permanent lender, 70, 71, 149, 151–153, 155–161, 209
   assignment of loan documents to, 209
   letter of assurances from, 90, 91, 156, 161
Permanent lender's attorney, 91, 151. See also Attorneys
Permanent loan commitment. See Permanent take-out commitment
Permanent take-out commitment, 3, 7, 23, 26, 34, 39, 44–45, 71, 73, generally Chapter 8, 176, 183, 185. See also Buy-sell/tripartite agreement
   assignment of, 89
   forms of, 7, 148–150
Personal guarantees. See Guarantees
Plans and specifications, 6, 22, 23, 32, 44, 69, 72, 76, 96, 153, 163, 192
   change orders, 44, 192
   fast-track construction, 76, 96, 163
   final, 69, 96
   preliminary, 23, 96
Plat, 91. See also Survey
Prebuys, 7, 148–150, 161. See also Permanent take-out commitment
Prime rate, 3. See also Interest rates
Problem loans, generally Chapter 10. See also Workouts
Projections. See Encroachments and projections
Promissory note, 86
Provider of take-out funds, 39, 45, 96, 165. See also Equity purchaser and Permanent lender
Punch list, 167

Real Estate Investment Trust (REIT), 1–4, 42, 190
Realtors, 24
Redemption, 190

INDEX

Regional shopping centers. *See* Shopping centers
Rehabs. *See* Alterations and additions
Reinsurance, 130–131. *See also* Title insurance
   1961 ALTA facultative reinsurance agreement, 131
   direct access agreement, 131
Rental achievement, 73
Replacement costs, 193. *See also* Costs
Representations and warranties, 53
Research and development (R&D) facilities. *See* Industrial space
Residential properties, 11, 13, 18–21, 37
   apartments, 13, 21
   condominiums, 13, 19, 21, 37
Restoration, 86, 87
Restrictive covenants, 41, 91
Retail space, 11. *See also* Shopping centers
Retainage, 38–40, 45, 72, 77, 167, 176
Retirement facilities, 18
Rights of way. *See* Easements
Riparian rights, 126

San Diego, California, 12
San Francisco, 14
San Jose, California, 12, 14
Savings Associations. *See* Banks
Seattle, Washington, 12
Security agreement, 88
Servicing. *See* Loan servicing
Shopping centers, 17, 19, 43. *See also* Leases
Soil reports. *See* Borings and soil reports
Soft costs. *See* Costs
Specific performance, 56
Spur track, 37
   agreement, 90, 155
Standby commitment, 151. *See also* Permanent take-out commitment
Standby financing, 191. *See also* Gap financing and Permanent financing
Strips and gores, 127
Subcontractors, 6, 132–133, 135–136, 185, 188, 192
   as mechanic's lien claimants, 132–133, 135–136, 185
   lien waivers from, 192
Subcontracts. *See* Construction contracts
Subordinated sale leaseback, 191

Subordinate lenders, 191
Subsurface rights, 121, 127
Sunbelt, 4, 12, 13, 19
Suppliers. *See* Subcontractors
Surety, 70, 98, 185. *See also* Guarantors
Survey, 70, 92, 121–123, 128, 152, 176
   certification, 70, 152
   final as-built, 176
   foundation, 70
   reports, 172
   title insurance coverage relating to, 128, 186
Syndications, 186, 191

Tax and Fiscal Responsibility Act of 1982 (TEFRA), 12. *See also* Taxes
Taxes, 8, 12, 19, 187, 189, 191
   affecting REITs, 1
   Economic Tax Recovery Act of 1981 (ERTA), 12
   flat tax, 19
   industrial development bonds, 8
   Tax and Fiscal Responsibility Act of 1982 (TEFRA), 12
Tax liens, 125
Tenant finish work, 32, 153. *See also* Leases
Tenants, 24, 35, 43. *See also* Leases
Termination date, 72
Texas, 4, 14, 131, 137
Theft and vandalism, 192. *See also* Materials
Title, 37, 120. *See also* Title insurance
   borrower's interest in the property, 37
   encumbrances on, 120–127
   fee simple, 37, 120
Title insurance, 41, 70, 120–131, 136–137, 174, 175, 185
   amount of, 129
   as protection against mechanics' liens, 41, 70, 124–125, 129–130, 136–137, 174–175, 185
   commitment for, 91
   coverage available, 120–129
   direct access agreement, 131
   policies, 125, 127, 129–130, 137
      assignment of, 127
      pending disbursements clause, 125
   reinsurance, 130–131

Title insurance companies, 41, 52, 91, 130, 136, 183, 190–192
   as disburser of loan proceeds, 41, 51, 135, 175–176
   construction loan escrow, 135
Title reports, 175–176, 183. *See also* Title insurance
Tripartite agreement. *See* Buy-sell/tripartite agreement
Truth in lending, 128

Uniform Commercial Code (UCC), 88
   financing statements, 88
   lien search, 88
Urban Development Action Grant (UDAG), 40
Urban Development Corporation (UDC), 40
Usury, 33–34, 37, 49–50, 87, 177–181, 186. *See also* Interest
   implications in guaranty to complete, 87
   opinion of borrower's counsel, 91
   title insurance protection, 128–129
Utilities, evidence of availability, 92

Vandalism. *See* Theft and vandalism

Warehouses, 37
Warranties. *See* Representations and warranties
Washington, D.C., 10, 131
Wiring instructions, 176
Wisconsin, 20
Workouts, 183–193
   a case study, 198–204

Zoning, 32, 40, 91, 152, 186
   title insurance protection, 129
   verification of compliance, 93